Psychological foundations of Education

Psychology

Intelligence

Personality

Adolescents Mental Health and Hygiene

Theories of Development

Zahoor Ahmad Thoker

Assistant Professor in Education

Govt. Degree College Kulgam

Shabeer Ahmad Bhat

Assistant Professor in Persian

Govt. Degree College Tral

Name of the book: Psychological foundations of Education

Authors: Zahoor Ahmad Thoker, Assistant Professor in Education Govt. Degree College Kulgam and Shabeer Ahmad Bhat, Assistant Professor in Persian Govt. Degree Colleg Tral

Year of publication: 2025

Pages: 214

Publisher: Notion publishing House

Price: 350

Preface

Psychological foundations of Education, is a book composed for the undergraduate course especially for 3rd semester. It also includes the chapters pertaining to B..ED, M. ED and P.G courses in Education. It was our passion to write a book for these semesters/courses keeping in view the NEP syllabus introduced recently in Jammu and Kashmir. The book is a masterpiece and will definitely help the students in their endeavours. The book is discussing the chapters including Psychology, Learning, Intelligence and IQ, Personality, Adolescents Mental Health and Hygiene and Theories of Development. The book was completed in 2023 but delayed in its publication because of mass transfer of college faculty in higher education due to the Elections of JK Assembly and Parliament Elections. Now with help of Shabeer Ahmad Bhat, Assistant Professor Persian Govt. Degree College

Tral, book was designed, necessary corrections done and made ready for its publication. It is expected that the book will be soon in the hands of our students. We express our sincere gratitude to our family, especially parents and friends.

Prof. Zahoor Ahmad Thoker, &
Prof. Shabeer Ahmad Bhat

Contents

Title	Page No
Psychology	1
Intelligence	56
Personality	94
Adolescents Mental Health and Hygiene	150
Theories of development	193

UNIT 1

Psychology

What is Psychology?

The word, 'Psychology' is derived from two Greek words, 'Psyche' and 'Logos'. Psyche means 'soul' and 'Logos' means 'science'. Thus psychology was first defined as the 'science of soul".

According to earlier psychologists, the function of psychology was to study the nature, origin and destiny of the human soul. But the soul is something metaphysical. It cannot be seen, observed and touched and we cannot make scientific experiments on the soul.

In the 18th century, psychology was understood as the 'Science of Mind'. William James (1892) defined psychology as the science of mental processes. But the word 'mind' is also quite ambiguous as there was confusion regarding the nature and functions of mind.

Modern psychologists defined psychology as the "Science of Consciousness". James Sully (1884) defined psychology as the "Science of the Inner World". Wilhelm Wundt (1892) defined psychology as the science which studies the "internal experiences'. But there are three levels of consciousness – conscious, subconscious and the unconscious and so this definition also was not accepted by some.

Thus psychology first lost its soul, then its mind and then its consciousness. At present only its behaviour exists. William McDugall (1905) defined psychology as the "Science of Behaviour", W.B. Pillsbury (1911) and J.B. Watson (1912) also defined psychology as the science of behaviour.

Behaviour generally means overt activities which can be observed and measured scientifically. But one's behaviour is always influenced by his experiences. So when we study one's behaviour we must also study his experiences.

Psychology should, therefore, be defined as a "science of behaviour and experiences on human beings" (B.F. Skinner)

According to Crow and Crow, "Psychology is the study of human behaviour and human relationship'.

Psychology is "the science of Behaviour and mental processes".

Psychology now is defined: Psychology is the scientific study of the mind and behaviour, according to the American Psychological Association. Psychology is a multifaceted discipline and includes many sub-fields of study such as human development, sports, health, clinical, social behaviour and cognitive processes.

What is Educational Psychology?

Educational psychology is that branch of psychology in which the findings of psychology are applied in the field of education. It is the scientific study of human behaviour in an educational setting.

According to Charles. E. Skinner, "Educational psychology deals with the behaviour of human beings in educational situations".

Thus educational psychology is a behavioural science with two main references– human behaviour and education.

In the words of E.A. Peel, "Educational Psychology is the science of Education".

Education by all means is an attempt to mould and shape the behaviour of the pupil. It aims to produce desirable changes in him for the all-round development of his personality.

The essential knowledge and skill to do this job satisfactorily is supplied by Educational Psychology. In the words of E.A. Peel, "Educational psychology helps the teacher to understand the development of his pupils, the range and limits of their capacities, the processes by which they learn and their social relationships."

In this way, the work of the Educational Psychologists resembles that of an Engineer, who is a technical expert. The Engineer supplies all the knowledge and skill essential for the accomplishment of the job satisfactorily... for example, construction of a bridge.

In the same way Educational Psychologists, who are technical experts in the field of Education, supply all the information, principles and techniques essential for understanding the behaviour of the pupil in response to the educational environment and desired modification of his behaviour to bring an all-round development of his personality.

In this way, it is quite reasonable to call Educational Psychology as a science and technology of Education.

Thus, Educational Psychology is concerned primarily with understanding the processes of teaching and learning that take place within formal environments and developing ways of improving those methods. It covers important topics like learning theories; teaching methods; motivation; cognitive, emotional, and moral development; and parent-child relationships etc.

In short, it is the scientific discipline that addresses the questions: "Why do some students learn more than others?" and "What can be done to improve that learning?"

NATURE OF EDUCATIONAL PSYCHOLOGY

Its nature is scientific as it has been accepted that it is a Science of Education. We can summarize the nature of Educational Psychology in the following ways:

1. Educational Psychology is a science. (Science is a branch of study concerned with observation of facts and establishment of verifiable general laws. Science employs certain objective methods for the collection of data. It has its objectives of understanding, explaining, predicting and controlling facts.) Like any other science, educational psychology has also developed objective methods of collection of data. It also aims at understanding, predicting and controlling human behaviour.

2. Educational Psychology is a natural science. An educational psychologist conducts his investigations, gathers his data and reaches his conclusions in exactly the same manner as physicists or the biologist.

3. Educational psychology is a social science. Like the sociologist, anthropologist, economist or political scientist, the educational psychologist studies human beings and their sociability.

4. Educational psychology is a positive science. Normative science like Logic or Ethics deals with facts as they ought to be. A positive science deals with facts as they are or as they operate. Educational psychology studies the child's behaviour as it is, not, as it ought to be. So it is a positive science.

5. Educational psychology is an applied science. It is the application of psychological principles in the field of education. By applying the principles and techniques of psychology, it tries to study the behaviour and experiences of the pupils. As a branch of psychology it is parallel to any other applied psychology. For example, educational psychology draws heavily from such areas as developmental psychology, clinical psychology, abnormal psychology and social psychology.

6. Educational psychology is a developing or growing science. It is concerned with new and ever new research. As research findings accumulate, educational psychologists get better insight into the child's nature and behaviour.

W.A. Kelly (1941) listed the nature of Educational Psychology as follows:

i. To give a knowledge of the nature of the child

ii. To give understanding of the nature, aims and purposes of education

iii. To give understanding of the scientific methods and procedures which have been used in arriving at the facts and principles of educational psychology

iv. To present the principles and techniques of learning and teaching

v. To give training in methods of measuring abilities and achievement in school subjects

vi. To give a knowledge of the growth and development of children

vii. To assist in the better adjustment of children and to help them to prevent maladjustment

viii. To study the educational significance and control of emotions and

ix. To give an understanding of the principles and techniques of correct training.

Thus, educational psychology is an applied, positive, social, specific and practical science. While general science deals with behaviour of the individuals in various spheres, educational psychology studies the behaviour of the individual in the educational sphere only.

SCOPE OF EDUCATIONAL PSYCHOLOGY

The scope of educational psychology is ever-growing due to constant research in this field. The following factors will indicate the scope of educational psychology:

1. The Learner. The subject-matter of educational psychology is knitted around the learner. Therefore, it is necessary to know the learner and the techniques of knowing him well. The topics include – the innate abilities and capacities of the individuals, individual differences and their measurements, the overt, covert, conscious as well as unconscious behaviour of the learner, the characteristics of his growth and development and each stage beginning from childhood to adulthood.

2. The Learning Experiences. Educational Psychology helps in deciding what learning experiences are desirable, at what stage of the growth and development of the learner, so that these experiences can be acquired with a greater ease and satisfaction.

3. Learning process: After knowing the learner and deciding what learning experiences are to be provided, Educational Psychology moves on to the laws, principles and theories of learning. Other items in the learning process are remembering and forgetting, perceiving, concept formation, thinking and reasoning, problem solving, transfer of learning, ways and means of effective learning etc.

4. Learning Situation or Environment. Here we deal with the environmental factors and learning situations which come midway between the learner and the teacher. Topics like classroom climate and group dynamics, techniques and aids that facilitate learning and evaluation, techniques and practices, guidance and counseling etc. for the smooth functioning of the teaching-learning process.

5. The Teacher: The teacher is a potent force in any scheme of teaching and learning process. It discusses the role of the teacher. It emphasizes the need of 'knowing thyself' for a teacher to play his role properly in the process of education. His conflicts, motivation. Anxiety, adjustment, level of aspiration etc. It throws light on the essential personality traits, interests, aptitudes, the characteristics of effective teaching etc so as to inspire him to become a successful teacher.

Though the entire scope of Educational Psychology is included in the above mentioned five key-factors, it may be further expanded by adding the following:

6. It studies Human Behaviour in educational situations. Psychology is the study of behaviour, and education deals with the modification of behaviour; hence, educational psychology pervades the whole field of education.

7. It studies the Growth and Development of the child. How a child passes through the various stages of growth and what are the characteristics of each stage are included in the study of educational psychology.

8. To what extent Heredity and Environment contribute towards the growth of the individual, and how this knowledge can be made use of for bringing about the optimum development of the child; form a salient feature of the scope of educational psychology.

9. Educational psychology deals with the Nature and Development of the Personality of an individual. In fact, education has been defined as the all-round development of the personality of an individual; personality development also implies a well-adjusted personality.

10. It studies Individual Difference: Every individual differs from every other individual. It is one of the fundamental facts of human nature which have been brought to light by educational psychology. This one fact has revolutionized the concept and process of education.

11. It studies nature Intelligence and its Measurement. This is of utmost importance for a teacher.

12. It Provides Guidance and Counseling: Education is nothing but providing guidance to the growing child.

We can conclude by saying that Educational Psychology is narrower in scope than general psychology. While general psychology deals with the behaviour of the individual in a general way, educational psychology is concerned with the behaviour of the learner in an educational setting.

Learning

The term learning is one of those concepts whose meaning is crystal clear until one has to put it in actual words. "Learning is when you learn something." "Learning is learning how to do something." The more useful definition is as follows: Learning is any relatively permanent change in behaviour brought about by experience or practice.

What does "relatively permanent" mean? And how does experience change what we do?

Relatively permanent part of the definition refers to the fact that when people learn something, some part of the brain is physically changed to record what they have learned. (Former et al., 2013) (Loftus and Loftus Loftus 1980). This is actually a process of memory, for without the ability to remember what happens, people cannot learn anything.

As for the inclusion of experience or practice in the definition of learning, think about the last time you did something that caused you a lot of pain. Did you do it again? Probably not. You did not want to experience that pain again, so you changed your behaviour to avoid the painful consequence. This is how children learn not to touch hot stoves. In contrast, if a person does something resulting in a very pleasurable experience, that person is more likely to do the same thing again. This is another change in behaviour and is explained by the law of effect, the topic we will discuss later in the chapter.

Not all change is accomplished through learning. Changes like an increase in height or the size of the brain are another kind of change, controlled by a genetic blueprint. This kind of change is called maturation and is due to Biology not experience. For example, practice alone will not allow a child to walk. Children learn to walk because their nervous system, muscle strength and sense balance has reached the point where walking is physically possible for them–all factors controlled by maturation. Once the maturation and readiness has been reached, then practice and experience plays an important role.

Definitions of learning

Gardner Murphy (1968)

The term learning covers every modification in behaviour to meet environmental requirements.

Henry P Smith (1962)

Learning is the acquisition of new behaviour or the strengthening or weakening of old behaviour as the result of experience.

Hilgard (1961)

Learning is a relatively permanent change in behavioural potentiality that occurs as a result of reinforced practice.

Crow and Crow (1973)

Learning is the acquisition of habits, knowledge and attitudes. It involves new ways of doing things and it operates in an individual's attempt to overcome obstacles or to adjust to new situations.

Pressey, Robinson And Horrocks (1967)

Learning is an episode in which a motivated individual attempts to adapt his behaviour so as to succeed in a situation which he perceives as requiring action to attain a goal.

Kingsley and R Gary (1957)

Learning is the process by which behaviour is originated or changes through practice or training.

Gales: defined Learning as the behavioural modification which occurs as a result of experience as well as training.

E.A, Peel, Learning can be described as a change in the individual which takes place as a result of the environmental change.

H.J.Klausmeir described Learning as a process which leads to some behavioural change as a result of some experience, training, observation, activity, etc.

Characteristics of learning

1. Learning is a process which is continuous and it never stops at any phase. It is a lifelong process. Hence learning starts from birth and ends only with the death of an individual. Hence we can say that learning proceeds from the womb to the tomb. For example when a child takes birth he first learns to cry for food, and at each phase of life, at every step the child learns To walk, Run, talk, write alphabets etc.

2. Learning is the process which leads to mental growth of an individual. The growth takes place along with the learning.

3. Basically when learning takes place the individual Learns to adjust and adapt with the environment.

4. Learning is purposeful. Though learning takes place at every place and at every moment all the learning is not useful. Hence those learning which are useful and meaningful are learnt.

5. Learning is an active process. Learning by doing is the best part of learning e.g. it becomes easy for the Science students to learn the concepts in science when they perform practical.

6. Learning takes place individually and as well as socially e.g. When a seminar or workshop is conducted, then all the members of the group learn to share their thoughts, each one learns something new from the other individual.

7. Learning brings about the change in the behaviour of an individual e.g. a child is always taught values and manners, and due to these teachings a child Learns to respect their elders and teachers, learn to speak politely etc. which brings about the change in his behaviour as the child grows.

Theories of learning **Trial and Error Theory**

Edward Lee Ted Thorndike (31st August 1874 -9 August 1949) was an American psychologist who developed learning theory that led to the development of operant conditioning within behaviourism.

Whereas, Classical conditioning depends on developing Association between events, Operant conditioning involves learning from the consequences of the behaviour. Skinner's theory of operant conditioning was built on the ideas of Edward Thorndike.

Thorndike was a Pioneer not only in behaviourism and in studying learning but also in using animals in psychology experiments.

Connectionism is a learning theory which is based on the concept of bonds formed between stimulus and response i.e., Natural connections between situations, and response are formed and strengthened. The stimulus affects the organism which responds to it.Thus S-R bonds are formed which are considered as physical conditions.

This theory of learning is related to conditioning that utilizes the concept of association of connection. It emphasizes that the behaviour begins with conditioned reflexes and natural responses and new behaviours result from the acquisition of new bonds through experience. Thorndike formulated the major laws of learning on the basis of his Belief in connectionism.

Thorndike's Puzzle Box

One of Thorndike's major contributions to the study of psychology was his work with animals.He believed that learning occurs through trial and error. The animal made many responses, many of them were wrong and ineffective and eventually learned to repeat those that got desirable results.

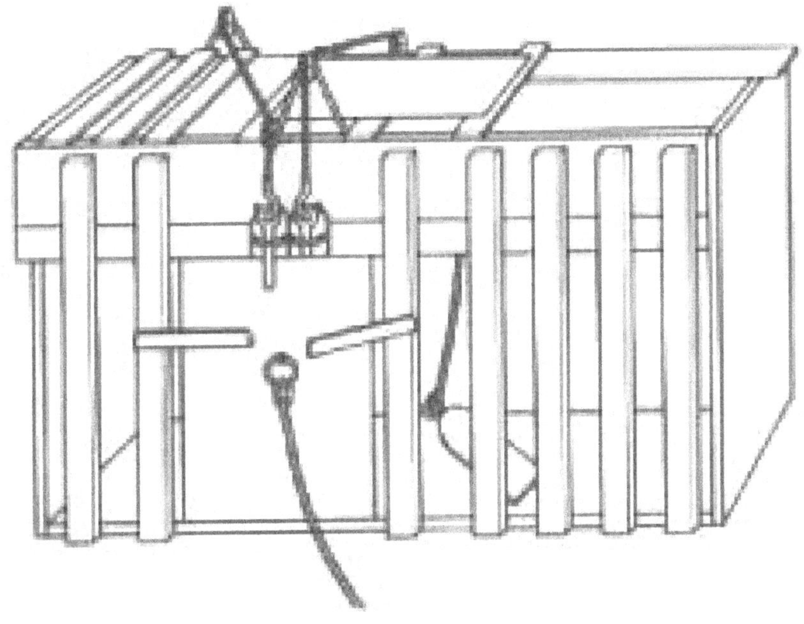

The puzzle box

Thorndike felt that learning was a matter of creating associations between stimulus and response and no speculation about mind was necessary or useful.Through long extensive research with these animals he constructed a device called puzzle box.

The puzzle box was approximately 20 inches long, 15 inches wide and 11 inches tall. The box had a door that was pulled open by a weight attached to a string that ran over a Pulley and was attached to the door. The string attached to the door led to a lever or button inside the box. When the animal pressed the bar or pulled the lever the string attached to the door would cause the weight to lift and the door to open. At first the cat was put in the cage, explored restlessly, but did not know how to escape. Eventually they stepped on the foot switch and the Trap door opened. On succeeding trials they operated the switch faster. Thorndike explained learning with his " law of effect." Animals tended to repeat a behaviour that resulted in a pleasing effect. This was an early version of the concept of positive reinforcement that skinner has used effectively. Behaviour was varied during a trial and error phase. Thorndike believed that the animal stumbled Upon a behaviour that produced a desirable effect.

This created a link between stimulus (cage) and response (stepping on switch or pulling the lever).Later in the same stimulus situation the response occurred faster. He produced a graph called a "Learning Curve" showing the number of seconds the animal had to escape on each trial.

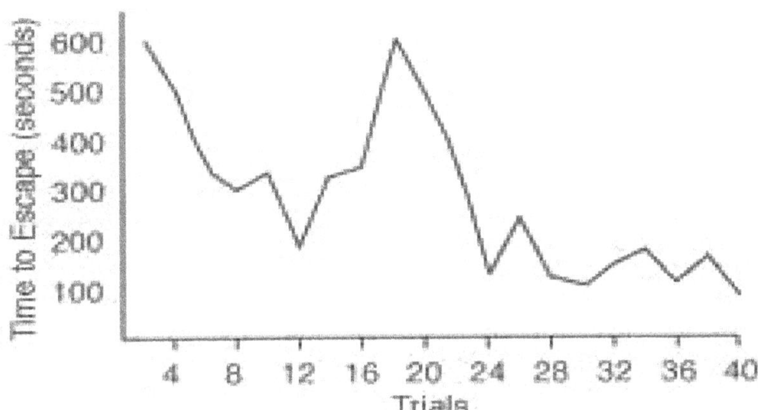

Learning curve

Thorndike concluded that all animals learn, solely by trial and error or reward and punishment. He used the cat's behaviour in the puzzle box to describe what happens when all the beings learn together.

All learning involves the formation of connection and connections were strengthened according to the law of effect. Intelligence is the ability to form connections and humans are the most evolved animal because they form more connections than any other being.

Thorndike's Laws

Thorndike presented the theory on laws of learning on the basis of his belief in connectionism. These laws are originally the outgrowth of experiments in the field of animal psychology. He first presented his theory in his book Animal learning published in 1898. The three major laws are:

1. Law of Readiness 2. Law of Exercise 3. Law of Effect.

Law of Readiness

"When a bond is ready to act, act gives satisfaction and not to act gives annoyance." If a person is ready to learn, he /she can learn quickly.

The law of readiness describes those situations in which the person who Learns either invites the object of his/her learning or rejects it. Readiness means a preparation of action. if a person is not prepared to learn, then learning cannot be instilled in him/her.

Readiness includes all those preparatory adjustments which immediately precede the activity. reminding the learner of his/her past experiences, the understanding of new things, diverting attention towards the subject to be learned, changing the environment to suit the learning are all included in readiness. The readiness creates a mental set for learning.

In Thorndike's view the law of readiness is active in three following conditions:

When the conduction unit is prepared to go into action, its work is quite satisfactory because nothing is done to alter it's working.

The inactivity of a conduction unit and any reaction may arise in connection with that deficiency.

When a conduction unit is forced to act while it is not prepared to do so, its behaviour is of a nature calculated to excite anger.

All these three characteristics describe the readiness for learning and is known by the tendency for learning in the learner. the tendency for learning results in self-contentment on learning. if the learning is obstructed even in the event of the presence of the tendency to learn then deep discontentment May result.

Thus, while on one hand the tendency towards learning is assistance in learning, it may be on the other hand can also be a source of discontentment in case, the learning is absent. In this way the law of readiness is related to mental preparation for action.

Law of exercise

The second important law has two aspects. It is based on the law of use and disuse. The law of use states "when a modifiable connection is made between a situation and a response that connection's strength is increased".

Similarly the law of disuse States, "when a modifiable connection is not made between a situation and response over a length of time, the connection's strength is decreased".

The repeated application of an activity fixes it firmly in the mind, while on the other hand, the relation is weakened through continuous disuse. Drill and practice helps in increasing efficiency and durability of learning. According to Thorndike's S-R bond theory, the connections are strengthened with trial and practice. Whenever, there is an appropriate situation the activity which is firmly entrenched, might take place. It is the experience that whenever any action is repeated, it becomes easy and prompts. Learning and relearning helps in mastering the activity. Repetition of activities fixes knowledge and skills to be learned. Practice makes it perfect. Lack of practice weakens memory and skills. It may be said that longer is the period of disuse greater is the loss of memory and weakening of skills.

Law of Effect

The meaning of the law of effect is the effect of learning. The trial or steps leading to satisfaction stamps in the bond or connection. Satisfying States leads to consolidation and strengthening of connection, whereas dissatisfaction, annoyance or pain lead to the weakening or Stamping out of the connection.

Success brings with it satisfaction and along with it a strengthening of the relation of the experience. Failure increases dissatisfaction and absence of the relation among the experiences weakens them.

The success can be compared to reward and failure to punishment, and the desire to repeat success or avoid failure as the inevitable antecedents.

Implications of the theory are the following:

1) The task can be started from the easier aspect towards its difficult aspect, which will help the children to learn properly.

2) Trial and error Method can be used in teaching

3) Rewards and punishments affect the learning of the child

4) Habits are formed as a result of repetition. Why with the help of

this theory the wrong habits can be modified and good habits can be strengthened.

5) Practice is the main feature of trial and error methods. It helps in reducing errors committed by children in learning a concept.

Theory of Classical Conditioning By Ivan Pavlov

Pavlo and the salivating dogs

Studying the digestive system in his dogs, Pavlov had built a device that would accurately measure the amount of saliva produced by the dogs when they were fed a measured amount of food. Normally when food is placed in the mouth of any animal, the salivary glands automatically start releasing saliva to help with chewing and digestion. This is a normal reflex — an unlearned, involuntary response that is not under personal control or choice — one of many that occur in both animals and humans. The food causes a particular reaction, salivation. A stimulus can be defined as any object, event, or experience that causes a response, the reaction of an organism. In the case of Pavlov's dogs, the food is the stimulus and salivation is the response.

Pavlov soon discovered that his dogs began salivating when they were not supposed to be salivating. Some dogs would start salivating when they saw the lab assistant bringing their food, others when they heard the clatter of the food bowl from the kitchen, and still others when it was the time of day they were usually fed. Switching his focus, Pavlov spent the rest of his career studying what eventually he termed classical conditioning, learning to elicit an involuntary, reflex –like response to a stimulus other than the original, natural stimulus that normally produces the response.

Elements of classical conditioning Pavlov eventually identified several key elements that must be present and experienced in a particular way for conditioning to take place.

Unconditioned stimulus: The original naturally occurring stimulus is called the unconditional stimulus (UCS). The term unconditioned means "unlearned." This is the stimulus that ordinarily leads to the involuntary response. In the case of a Pavlov's dogs, the food is the unconditional stimulus.

Unconditional response The Automatic and involuntary response to the unconditional stimulus is called the unconditional response(UCR) for much the same reason it is unlearned and occurs because of genetic "wiring" in the nervous system. For example in Pavlov's experiment the salivation to the food is the

UCR(unconditioned response).

Conditioned stimulus Pavlov determined that almost any kind of stimulus could become associated with the unconditioned stimulus (UCS) if it is paired with the unconditioned stimulus often enough. In his original study the site of the food dish itself became a stimulus for salivation before the food was given to the dogs.Every time they got food (to which they automatically salivated) they saw the dish. At this point the dish was a neutral stimulus(NS) because it had no effect on salivation. After being paired with the food so many times, the dish came to produce a salivation response, although a somewhat weaker one, as did the food itself. When a previously neutral stimulus through repeated pairing with the unconditioned stimulus begins to cause the same kind of involuntary response, learning has occurred. The previously neutral stimulus can now be called a conditioned stimulus (CS). (Conditioned means "learned" and, as mentioned earlier, unconditioned means "unlearned").

Conditioned response: The response that is given to the CS (conditioned stimulus) is not usually quite as strong as the original unconditioned response (UCR), but it is essentially the same response. However because it comes as a learned response to the conditioned stimulus (CS), it is called the conditioned response (CR).

 Putting it all together Pavlos Canine Classic, or Tick Tok Tick Tok

 Pavlov did a classic experiment in which he paired the ticking sound of a metronome (a simple device that produces a rhythmic ticking sound) with the presentation of food to see if the dogs would eventually salivate at the sound of the metronome (Pavlov,1927). Since the metronome ticking did not normally produce salivation, it was a neutral stimulus (NS),before any conditioning took place. The repeated pairing of an NS and the UCS (unconditional stimulus) is usually called acquisition because the organism is in the process of acquiring learning.

Notice that the responses, CR (conditioned response) and UCR (unconditioned response) are very similar –salivation. However, they differ not only in strength but also in the stimulus to which they are the response. An unconditioned stimulus (UCS) is always followed by an unconditioned response (UCR) and a conditioned stimulus (CS) is always followed by a conditioned response (CR).

Classical conditioning is actually one of the simplest forms of learning. It is so simple that it happens to people all the time without them even being aware of it. Does your mouth water when you merely see an advertisement for your favorite food on television? Do you feel anxious every time you hear the high-pitched whine of the dentist's drill? These are both examples of classical conditioning. Over the course of many visits to the dentist, for example the body comes to associate that sound(CS) with the anxiety or fear (UCR) the person has felt while receiving a painful dental treatment (UCS) and so the sound produces a feeling of anxiety(CR) whether that person is in the chair or just in the outer waiting area.

Pavlov and his fellow researchers did many experiments with the dogs in addition to the metronome, whistles, tuning forks, various visual stimuli and bells were used (Thomas 1994). Although classical conditioning happens quite easily, Pavlov and his other researchers formulated a few basic principles about the process. (Although we will see that there are a few exceptions to some of these principles):

Principles of Classical Conditioning

1 The CS must come before the UCS. If Pavlov sounded the metronome just after he gave the dogs the food, they did not

become conditioned (Rescorla1988).

2 The CS and UCS must come very close together in time–ideally, no more than 5 seconds apart. When Pavlov tried to stretch the time between the potential CS and the UCS to several minutes no Association or link between the two was made.

3 The neutral stimulus must be paired with the UCS several times and many times before conditioning takes place (Pavlov1926).

4 The CS is usually some stimulus that is distinctive or stands out from other competing stimuli. The metronome for example was a sound that was not normally present in the laboratory and therefore distinct (Pavlov 1927 Rescorla 1988).

Operant Conditioning by Skinner:

BF Skinner (1904 1990) was the behaviourist Who assumed leadership of the field after John Watson he was even more determined then Watson that psychologist should study only measurable observable behaviour in addition to his knowledge of pavlovian classical conditioning signature found in the work of thorndike a way to explain all behaviour as the product of learning he will give the learning of voluntary behaviour a special name operant conditioning Skinner 1938 voluntary behaviour is what people and animal is do to operate in the world people perform a voluntary action it is to get something that they want or to avoid something they do not want right so voluntary Behaviour for signature is operant behaviour and the learning of such behaviour is operant conditioning

The heart of operant conditioning is the effect of consequences on behaviour. Thinking back to the section on classical conditioning, learning an involuntary behaviour really depends on what comes before the response, the unconditioned stimulus and what will become the conditioned stimulus. These two are the antecedent stimuli (antecedent meaning is something that comes before another thing). But in operant conditioning learning depends on what happens after the response---the consequence.In a way operant conditioning could be summed up as this "if I do this, what is in it for me?".

The nature of Operant Conditioning: Consequential Operations

In situations involving operant conditioning the probability that a given behaviour will occur depending on the consequences that follow it. Psychologists generally agree that these probabilities are determined through four basic procedures, two of which strengthen or increase the rate of behaviour and two of which weaken or decrease the rate of behaviour. Procedures that strengthen behaviour are termed reinforcement whereas those that suppress behaviour are termed punishment.

Reinforcement

There are two types of reinforcement: Positive reinforcement and Negative Reinforcement. Positive reinforcement involves the impact of positive reinforcers — stimulus events or consequences that strengthen responses that precede them. In other words if a consequence of some action increases the probability that the action will occur again in the future, that consequence is functioning as a positive reinforcer. Some positive reinforcers seem to exert these effects because they are related to basic biological needs. Such primary reinforcers include food when we are hungry, water when we are thirsty and sexual pleasure. In contrast other events acquire their capacity to act as positive reinforcers through association with primary reinforcers.

Preferred activities can also be used to reinforce behaviour, a principle referred to as premack principle. If you recall hearing "you must clean your room before you can watch TV" or "you must eat your vegetables before you get dessert" when you were growing up then you are already familiar with this principle. As you can guess the premack principle is a powerful tool for changing behaviour.

Please note that a stimulus event that functions as a positive reinforcer at one time or in one context, may have a different effect at another time, or another place. Example food may serve as a positive reinforcer when you are hungry but not when you are ill or just after you finish a large meal.

Negative reinforcement involves the impact of negative reinforcement—stimuli that strengthen responses that permit an organism to avoid or escape from their presence. Thus when we perform an action that allows us to escape from a negative reinforcer that is already present or to avoid the threatened application of one, our tendency to perform this action in the future increases.

There are many examples of negative reinforcement in our everyday lives. To illustrate this imagine the following scene on a particular cold and dark winter morning when you are sleeping soundly in a warm comfortable bed suddenly the alarm clock across the room begins to wail. Getting out of your cozy bed is the last thing you want to do, but you find the noise intolerable. What do you do? if you get up to turn off the alarm—or, on subsequent Mornings get up early to avoid hearing the sound of the alarm altogether. Your behaviour has been negative reinforcement in other words your tendency to perform actions that allow you to escape from or avoid the sound of the alarm clock has increased. Another everyday example of negative reinforcement occurs when parents give into their children's tantrums–especially in public places, such as restaurants and shopping malls. Over time the parents' tendency to give in may increase, because doing so stops the screaming. To repeat them, both positive and negative reinforcements are procedures that strengthen or increase behaviour. Positive reinforcers are stimulus events that strengthen responses that precede them, whereas negative reinforcers are aversive(unpleasant)stimulus events that strengthen responses that lead to their termination or avoidance.

Punishment

In contrast to reinforcement punishment refers to procedures that weaken or decrease the rate of behaviour. As with reinforcement there are two types of punishment: positive punishment and negative punishment. In positive punishment behaviours are followed by aversive stimulus events termed punishers. In such instances we learn not to perform these actions because aversive consequences—punishers—will follow.

In negative punishment The rate of a behaviour is weakened or decreased because the behaviour is linked to the loss of potential reinforcements (Catania 1992 Melanson and Leslie 1979). For example parents frequently attempt to decrease the frequency of certain behaviours of their teenagers. For example hitting younger siblings or talking back to parents by temporarily denying the teenagers access to positive reinforcers such as driving the family car on weekend dates.Negative punishment is also commonly referred to as "time out" a procedure you may have experienced as a youngster growing up. Thus both positive and negative punishment are procedures that weaken or decrease behaviour.

Operant Conditioning Some Basic Principles

Shaping and Chaining: Getting behaviour started and then putting it all together

Many of the behaviours that we perform each day require little conscious effort on our part. But what about new forms of behaviour with which we are unfamiliar? How are these behaviours initially established? The answer involves a procedure known as shipping, A technique in which closer and closer approximations to desired behaviour are required for the delivery of positive reinforcement.

In essence shaping is based on the principle that a little can eventually go a long way.The organism undergoing shaping receives a reward for each small step towards a final goal—the target response—rather than all the for the final response. At first actions even remotely resembling the target behaviour—termed successive approximations -- are followed by a reward gradually, and closer and closer approximations of the final target behaviour are required before the award is given. Shaping then, helps organisms acquire, or construct new and more Complex forms of behaviour from simpler behaviour.

What about even more Complex sequences of behaviour, such as routines performed by Circus animals? These behaviours can be cultivated by means of a particular procedure called chaining, a procedure that establishes a sequence of responses, which lead to a reward following the final response in the chain.

Schedules of Reinforcement

Skinner put forward the idea of planning of schedules of reinforcement for conditioning the operant behaviour of the organism. Some important schedules are:

1 Continuous reinforcement schedule

This is an out and out reinforcement schedule where provision is made to reinforce or reward every correct response of the organism during acquisition of a learning. For example a student may be rewarded for every correct answer he gives to the question or problems put forth by the teacher.

2 Fixed interval reinforcement schedule: In this schedule the organism is rewarded for a response made only after a set interval of time for example every 3 minutes or every 5 minutes. It is only at the expiry of the fixed interval that he is presented with some reinforcement

3 Fixed ratio reinforcement schedule: In this schedule the reinforcement is given after a fixed number of responses. A rat for example might be given a pellet of food after a certain number of lever presses, a student may be probably rewarded after he answers a fixed number of questions, say 3 or 5.

4 Variable reinforcement schedules: When reinforcement is given at varying intervals of time or after a varying number of responses. It is called a variable reinforcement schedule. In this case reinforcement is intermittent or irregular, the individual does not know when he is going to be rewarded and consequently he remains motivated throughout the learning process in the hope of reinforcement. The most common example of such a schedule in human behaviour is the reinforcement operation schedule of gambling devices. Here rewards are unpredictable and keep the players well motivated through occasional returns.

Observational learning

Learning from the behaviour and outcomes of others

While at a formal dinner party, you notice five different forks, placed next to your plate, including two of a shape you have never seen before. Which ones do you use for which dishes? You have no idea. In order to avoid making a complete fool of yourself, as the first course arrives, you watch the other guests. When several reach unhesitatingly for one of the unfamiliar forks, you do the same. Now thank goodness, you can concentrate on the food.

You have probably encountered a similar situation, in which you have acquired new information, forms of behaviour or even abstract rules and concepts from watching the actions of other people and the consequences they experience. Such observational learning is a third major way we learn, and it is a common part of everyday life. (Bandura 1977, 1986). Indeed a large body of research findings suggest it can play a role in almost every aspect of behaviour.

More formal evidence for the existence of observational learning has been provided by hundreds of studies, many of them were performed with children. Perhaps the most famous of these studies are the well-known "Bobo doll" experiment conducted by Bandura and his colleagues (e.g.,Bandura,Ross and Ross 1963). In these studies one group of nursery school children saw an adult engage in aggressive actions against a large inflated Bobo doll. The adult who was serving as a model knocked the doll down, sat on It, insulted it verbally and repeatedly punched it in the nose. Another group of children were exposed to a model, who behaved in a non aggressive manner. Later both groups of youngsters were placed in a room with several toys, including a Bobo doll. Careful observation of their behaviour revealed that those who had seen the aggressive adult model, often imitated this person's behaviour. They too punched the toy, sat on it and even uttered verbal comments, similar to those of the model. In contrast children in the control group rarely if ever demonstrated such actions. While you may not find these results surprising, they may be significant in relation to the enduring controversy over whether children acquire new ways of aggression through exposure to violent television programs and movies. We will return to this issue shortly for the moment, let's consider the nature of observational learning itself.

Observational learning: some basic principles:

Given that observational learning exists, what factors and conditions determine whether, and to what extent we acquire behaviours, information or concepts from others? The following four factors appear to be the most important (Bandura 1986).

First in order to learn through observation you must direct your attention to appropriate models—-that is to other persons performing an activity. And, as you might expect, you don't choose such models at random but focus most attention on people who are attractive to you; on people who possess signs that they know what they are doing, such as status or success and on people whose behaviour seems relevant to your own needs and goals(Barren 1970).

Second, you must be able to remember what the person has said or done. Only if you can retain some representation of their actions in memory, can you perform similar actions at later times or acquire Useful information from them.

Third, you need to be able to convert these memory representations into appropriate action. This aspect of observational learning is termed the production process. Production process depends on (1) your own physical abilities—if you cannot perform the behaviour in question, having a clear picture of it in memory is of little use; (2) your capacity to monitor your own performance and adjust it, until it matches that of the model.

Finally motivation plays a role. We often acquire information through observational learning but do not put it into immediate use in our own behaviour. You may have no need for the information, as when you watch someone tie a bow tie but have no plans to wear one yourself. Or the observed behaviour may involve high risk of punishment or be repugnant to you personally, as when you observe an ingenious way of cheating during an exam but do not want to try it yourself. Only if the information or behaviours acquired are useful will observers put them to actual use.

As you can see, observational learning is a complex process—far more Complex than mere imitation—and plays an important role in many aspects of behaviour. This point is perhaps most forcefully illustrated by a controversy that has persisted in psychology and in society as a whole since the early 1960: the controversy over whether children and perhaps even adults are made more aggressive by long-term exposure to violence on television shows or in movies.

Theory of Learning by Insight:

This theory is also called Gestalt Theory of Learning. An explanation of Gestalt School of Psychology: The word Gestalt in German means 'whole', 'total pattern' or 'configuration'. This school believes that the whole is more important than the parts. So learning also takes place as a whole'. In this respect Kohlar performed a number of experiments on monkeys, and arrived at the result that the highest type of learning is through insight.

Learning by insight means sudden grasping of the solution, a flash of understanding, without any process of trial and error. All discoveries and inventions have taken place through insight. Of course the discoverer possessed a complete knowledge of the whole situation in peace-meal.

The Gestalt psychologists dismiss the theory of 'trial and error'; hit and miss' strive and succeed'. Another modern psychologist E.C. Tolman also rejects the trial and error theory and approaches the insight theory.

According to Tolman, in all learning some intelligence is at work. It is the learner who actively participates in the act of getting new experience. He organizes his perceptions and observations and gives meaning to them. It is his whole mind that perceives, constructs and reconstructs experience. In his 'purposive theory of learning', he explains the behaviour or rats in teaching the goal through many trials as a result of 'insight' or 'making cognitive map' of the maze.

Experiments of Theory of Learning by Insight:

(I) Kohler's experiment on Sultan (Experiment with box):

Kohler kept a monkey (named Sultan) hungry for some time, and then shut him in a large cage. He hung bananas from the ceiling, and kept a box on the floor of the cage, fast beneath. The monkey could not reach the banana. Another box was put in a corner of the cage.

But the Sultan could not get the idea of placing one box on the other and thus reaching the banana. Ultimately Kohlar gave a demonstration of putting one box on the other. The Sultan could now learn the whole situation. He used his intelligence and insight to put the two boxes one upon the other, stand on these and then reach the bananas.

(ii) **Experiment with two sticks:**

In another experiment Kohler kept two sticks in the cage. One end of the shorter sticks could be fitted in the one end of the longer sticks, so as to make them longer. The monkey did not get the idea of forming the two sticks through trial and error. When Kohlar gave a hint through putting his finger in the hole of the bigger stick, the monkey viewed the whole situation and performed the right task through understanding the insight.

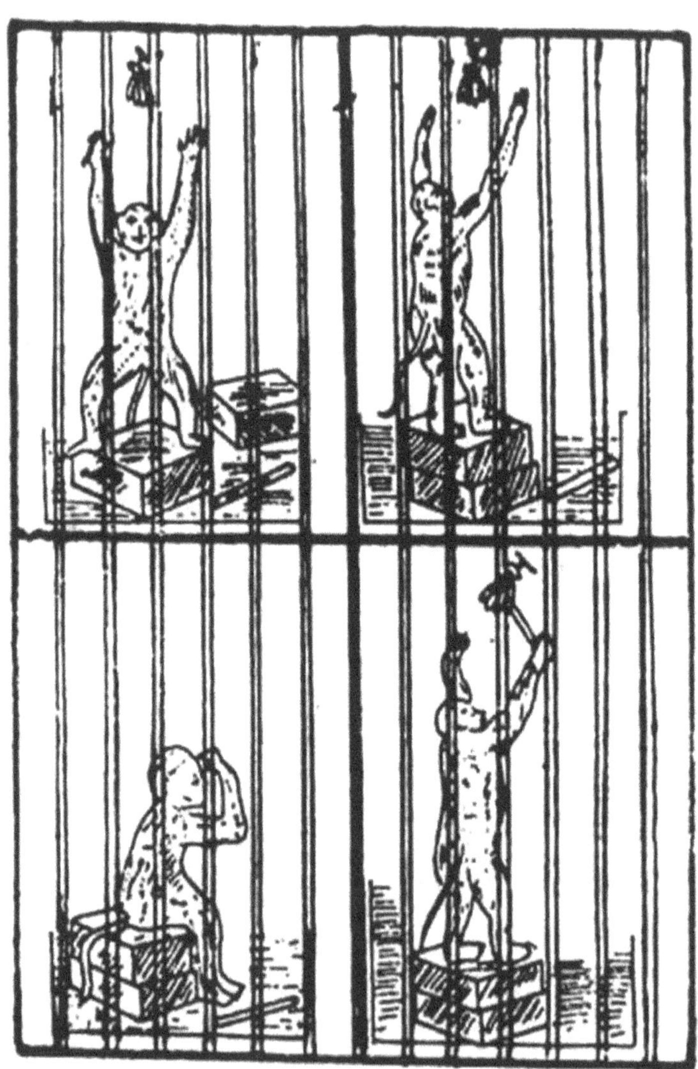

Fig. Kohler's experiment on chimpanzee.

Criterion or Essentials of Learning by Insight:

1. Comprehension as a whole:

Learning by insight requires full comprehension of the situation as a whole.

2. Clear goal:

The goal must be quite clear to begin with.

3. Power of generalisation:

The learner must possess the power of generalisation along with those of differentiation.

4. Suddenness of solution:

Suddenness of the solution is the hallmark of learning by insight i.e., the solution flashes suddenly to the learner. No lengthy reasoning is involved.

5. New forms of objects:

As a result of insight into the problem or situation objects appear in new forms and patterns.

6. Transfer:

Transfer of learning occurs as a result of insight. The principles learnt in one situation are applied to the other situation.

7. Change in behaviour:

Insight changes our behaviour to the extent which we have learnt through insight.

Laws of Insight Formation:

1. Capacities:

Insight depends upon the capacity of the organism. Individuals offer in their capacities. The more developed the individual, the more will be the capacity to develop insight.

2. Previous experience:

Insight depends upon relevant previous experience and maturation. Some practice, trial and error and maturation up to the level is essential before insight develops. A child of five years cannot develop mathematical insight since he has not done sufficient practice in it.

3. Experimental arrangement:

Development of insight depends upon experimental arrangement also.

4. Fumbling and search:

Insight follows a period of fumbling and search.

5. Readily repeated:

Insightful solutions can be readily repeated.

6. Use in new situation:

Insight once achieved can be used in new situations.

7. Wholesome experience:

Experience of insight is always wholesome. Whole is just not equal to its parts.

Educational Implications of Learning by Insight (Role of Teacher in Insight Learning):

1. Integrated curriculum:

The curriculum of the class should be an integrated whole i.e., there should be correlation between various subjects.

2. Problem as a whole:

The whole problem is to be presented in the class. A piecemeal approach will not develop learning by insight. This theory believes, "The whole is not a sum of the parts." The teacher should present the things in the class as a whole atleast to start with. To give a complete insight into the learning material, we should always proceed from whole to the part. The lesson should form an integrated unit because insight is possible if the situation is perceived as a whole.

(i) The whole sentence should be presented first and then analyzed into words or letters.

(ii) While teaching Biology, the model of the whole body should be presented before the children and then the various parts and organs of the body should be emphasized.

(iii) While teaching geography, we should part from the globe and then come down to country, state, district and city.

3. Child as a whole:

Parents and teachers should see the child as a whole and in total setting. It is not wise to conclude on the basis of a single act about the child's behaviour.

4. Importance of motivation:

The theory stresses the importance of motivation in learning. Therefore, the teacher should motivate the students properly for insightful learning.

5. Importance of transfer:

The theory also emphasizes the importance of transfer of learning. Previous experiences are helpful in learning. Hence the teacher should encourage the students to make the best use of transfer of learning.

6. Emphasis on intelligent learning:

The theory is economical in terms of human energy. It puts emphasis on insight and understanding rather than rote learning. So spoon feeding and cramming should be discouraged. There are no useless and random efforts. The teacher should encourage the students to learn by understanding and insight i.e., intelligence.

7. Development of higher mental faculties:

Insight involves the maximum use of intelligence. Therefore, learning by insight is helpful in developing and improving higher mental processes like thinking, imagination, reasoning, analytical ability, problem solving, creativity etc. The theory specially encourages creative activity of the child. The teacher has to view the situation as a whole and then decide the line of action.

8. Problem solving approach:

Insight helps in solving problems through one's own efforts. This approach trains the child to solve his problems in life. Therefore, the teacher should make use of problem solving approaches for better learning. He should prepare children emotionally and intellectually to solve the problem.

9. Useful for difficult subjects:

The theory is especially useful for learning difficult subjects like science, mathematics and literature.

10. Useful for scientific inventions:

The theory is very useful for scientific inventions and discoveries.

11. Individual differences:

(a) The teacher keeps in mind the intelligence level, maturity and other types of individual differences. Intelligence plays a major role in learning by insight. The more intelligent a child is, the more he will learn through insight. The less intelligent child takes more time and makes more efforts to gain insight.

(b) Insight of the child should be carefully handled by the teacher. He should know that its development is related to the physical maturation of the child. He should present the problem as per the child.

12. Logical presentation:

The teacher should present his lesson logically. He should proceed from 'simple to complex', 'concrete to abstract', 'empirical to rational' and 'psychological to logical'. The problems presented in the class should be linked with life so that the learners have the greatest benefit out of them.

13. Persistent efforts:

It needs a lot of patience on the part of the teacher. Insight does not develop in the learner immediately. It needs persistent efforts.

14. Goal-oriented approach:

The teacher should develop in the learner the purpose of striving towards a goal on the basis of the child's experience. He should relate the topic taught to the experiences of the child and then lead him towards the goal.

15. Multiple approaches:

Ability of the learner and his past experiences play an important role in insight.

In 1956,the American educational psychologist Robert M. Gagné proposed a system of classifying different types of learning in terms of the degree of complexity of the mental processes involved. He identified eight basic types, and arranged these in the hierarchy shown in Figure 1. According to Gagné, the higher orders of learning in this hierarchy build upon the lower levels, requiring progressively greater amounts of previous learning for their success. The lowest four orders tend to focus on the more behavioural aspects of learning, while the highest four focus on the more cognitive aspects.

HIERARCHY OF LEARNING

Learning has been defined as a relatively permanent change in a behavioral tendency, the result of reinforced practice. Learning, an inferred state of an organism, should be distinguished from performance, an observed state of the organism, should be distinguished from performance, an observed state of the organism. Learning events consist of stimuli, learner and responses.

The most complete description of Gagne's classes of behaviour appears in his 'The conditions of learning'. Here he distinguishes eight types of learning, beginning with the simple forms and ending with the complex. Although he refers to these classes as learning types, he is primarily interested in the observable behaviour and performance which were the products of each such class.

| PROBLEM SOLVING |
| RULE LEARNING |
| CONCEPT LEARNING |
| DISCRIMINATION LEARNING |
| VERBAL ASSOCIATIN |
| CHAINING |
| STIMULUS RESPONSE LEARNING |
| SIGNAL LEARNING |

Signal learning

This is the simplest form of learning, and consists essentially of the classical conditioning first described by the behavioural psychologist Pavlov. IIn this type of learning the animal or individual acquires a conditioned response to a given signal. Pavlov studied such learning in great detail. In it the responses are diffuse and emotional and the learning is involuntary. Examples are the withdrawal of the hand upon sight of a hot object, the salivation of a dog upon hearing food poured into his metal feeding dish, and the tearing of the eyes upon sight of an onion . The signals are the sight of the hot object, the sound of food being poured in the dish, and the sight of the onion. The conditioned responses are withdrawal of the hand, salivation, and tearing of the eyes.

Stimulus-response learning

This somewhat more sophisticated form of learning, which is also known as operant conditioning, was originally developed by Skinner.In this kind of learning, exemplified by animal training, the animal makes precise responses to specific stimuli. At first this training usually requires the use of a leash and a choke chain. As the dog learns particular responses for particular jerks of the leash and chain, his master rewards him with pats and praise. Later the master does not have to use the leash and chain; the animal sits, stays, or lies down upon hearing the simple verbal command. Whereas the responses in signal learning are diffuse and emotional, the responses in stimulus-response learning (often called operant conditioning) are fairly precise. Stimulus-response (SàR) learning may be used in acquiring verbal skills as well as physical movements. For example , the child may learn to say "Mama" on request, or an adult may learn the appropriate response to the stimulus of a word in a foreign language.

Chaining

This is a more advanced form of learning in which the subject develops the ability to connect two or more previously-learned stimulus-response bonds into a linked sequence. It is the process whereby most complex psychomotor skills (eg riding a bicycle or playing the piano) are learned.In this type of learning the person links together previously learned S-R's. The links may involve physical reactions such as an animal learning a series of tricks, each of which gives the cue to perform the next trick.This type of learning often seems to occur so naturally that we do not notice the specific series of events which led to it. Gagne uses the example of a child who learns to say "doll" at the sight of a doll, then learns to lie down, hug the doll, and say "doll".

Verbal association

This is a form of chaining in which the links between the items being connected are verbal in nature. Verbal association is one of the key processes in the development of language skills.This learning is a type of chaining, but the links are verbal units. The simplest verbal association is the activity of naming an object, which involves a chain of two links: An observing response enables the child to properly identify the object he sees; and an internal stimulus enables the child to say the proper name. When the child can name an object "ball" and also say " the red ball" he has learned a vernal association of three links. Gagne calls another common verbal association translation responses; in these the learner frequently acquires verbal associations by verbal mediation- an internal link which helps him associate.

Discrimination learning

This involves developing the ability to make appropriate (different) responses to a series of similar stimuli that differ in a systematic way. The process is made more complex (and hence more difficult) by the phenomenon of interference, whereby one piece of learning inhibits another. Interference is thought to be one of the main causes of forgetting.In this type of learning the student must learn different responses for stimuli which might be confused. The student learns to distinguish between motor and verbal chains he has already acquired. Teachers, Gagne suggests, engage in discrimination learning when the device means for calling each student by his correct name.

Concept learning

This involves developing the ability to make a consistent response to different stimuli that form a common class or category of some sort. It forms the basis of the ability to generalize, classify etc. in learning a concept we respond to stimuli in terms of abstract characteristics like color, shape, position and number as opposed to concrete physical properties like specific wavelengths or particular intensities. In concept learning the student's behaviour is not under the control of particular physical stimuli but of the abstract properties of each stimulus. Concepts have concrete references even though they are learned with the use of language.

Rule learning

This is a very-high-level cognitive process that involves being able to learn relationships between concepts and apply these relationships in different situations, including situations not previously encountered. It forms the basis of the learning of general rules, procedures, etc.In learning a rule we relate two or more concepts. Rules are, in effect, chains of concepts. We may represent knowledge as a hierarchy of rules, in which we must learn two or more rules before learning a higher order rule which embraces them. If the student has learned the component concepts and rules, the teacher can use verbal instruction alone in leading the student to put the rules together.

Problem solving

This is the highest level of cognitive process according to Gagné. It involves developing the ability to invent a complex rule, algorithm or procedure for the purpose of solving one particular problem, and then using the method to solve other problems of a similar nature.

In the set of events called problem solving, individuals use rules to achieve some goal. When the goal is reached, however, the student has learned something more and is then capable of new performances using his new knowledge. What is learned is a higher order rule, the combined product of two or more lower order rules. Thus problem solving requires those internal events usually called thinking.. Without knowledge of the prerequisite rules, the problem can not be solved.

Glossary of terms

Psychology: Psychology is the scientific study of the mind and behaviour.

Educational Psychology: it is the field that studies and applies theories and concepts from all of psychology in educational settings.

Learning: Learning is a relatively permanent change in behaviour (or behaviour potential) brought about by experience.

Maturation: A basic biological process within which a person from time to time manifests different traits, the blueprints of which have been carried in his cells.

Reflex: An involuntary response, one that is not under personal control or choice.

Conditioning: Learning to make an involuntary response to a stimulus other than original, natural stimulus that normally produces the response.

Stimulus Generalisation: The tendency to respond to a stimulus that is only similar to a conditioned stimulus with the conditioned stimulus.

Stimulus Discrimination: The tendency to stop making a generalized response to a stimulus that is similar to the original conditioned stimulus.

Acquisition: The process by which a conditioned stimulus acquires the ability to elicit a conditioned response through repeated pairings of an unconditioned stimulus with the conditioned stimulus.

Extinction: The disappearance or weakening of a learned response following the removal or absence of the unconditioned stimulus.

Spontaneous Recovery: The reappearance of a learned response after extinction has occurred.

Vicarious Conditioning: Classical Conditioning of an involuntary response or emotion by watching the reaction of another person.

Operant Conditioning: The learning of voluntary behaviour through the effect of pleasant and unpleasant consequences to responses.

Operant: Any behaviour that is voluntary and not elicited by specific stimuli.

Reinforcement: Any event or stimulus that when following a response, increases the probability that the response will occur again.

Punishment: Any event or object that, when following a response, makes the response less likely to happen again.

Observational Learning: Learning new behaviour by watching a model performs that behaviour.

Insight: means sudden grasping of the solution, a flash of understanding, without any process of trial and error.

UNIT II

Intelligence

Intelligence and IQ

The most important variable that affects schooling or performance on a job is intelligence.

Psychologists have interpreted the term intelligence in different ways, and there is no consensus among them on the term even so far.

In psychology this term is treated as a "construct" whose structure is different in different individuals. The vagueness of the term arises due to the fact that intelligence is not a concrete material, it is abstracted from the behaviour of an individual which is indirectly inferred and elaborated as an adjective.

Dictionary meaning of Intelligence is "capacity to acquire and apply knowledge".

Boring defines intelligence as "intelligence is what intelligence tests measure".

Definitions of Intelligence

Several psychologists have classified and defined intelligence in several ways, some of them are given below:

1 Biological approach (vernon's classification)

Man is an organism among millions of organisms living on earth. Environment acts as a foe for him, intelligence is the capacity to adapt to the environment or new situations of life at every moment.

2 psychological approach According to psychologists intelligence is a relative effect of heredity and environment both.

3 Operational approach this definition helps us to understand the concept of Intelligence in clear and definite terms. In this approach scientific terms are defined operationally. and then observations are conducted with reference to these terms, for example in order to determine IQ we first Administer a test of a specific kind, then we observe his performance on the test and draw certain conclusions in context of pre–determined objectives.

Freemans classification Ability of adjustment: an individual is intelligent to the extent to which he is able to adjust to new situations and problems of life.

Ability to learn is also an index of Intelligence.

Ability to carry out abstract thinking

According to Termanan, an individual is intelligent to the extent he is able to carry on abstract thinking.

E.L.Thorndike intelligence as a global capacity

A comprehensive definition of Intelligence by Wechsler and Stoddard is as under:

Intelligence is the aggregate or global capacity of an individual to act purposefully, to think rationally and to deal effectively with one's environment.

Today, Intelligence is generally understood as, The ability to understand and adapt to the environment by using inherited abilities and learned knowledge.

IQ the term IQ was given by William Stern for Ratio between mental age and chronological age.

$IQ = M.A \div C.A \times 100$

The concept of mental age was given by Alfred Binet. Alfred Binet is regarded as the father of intelligence test construction.

Two Factor Theory of Intelligence by Charles Spearman

Two factor theory developed by an English Psychologist Charles Spearman in 1904. According to him, intellectual abilities consist of two factors: general ability known as 'G' and specific abilities known as 'S' factor.

Characteristics of G

1.It is a universal inborn ability.

2. It is a general mental ability.

3. It is constant (i.e.) it remains the same in all the individuals and does   not change with time.

4. Amount of 'G' differs from person to person depending on his genes

5. It is used in every life activity.

6. Greater the amount of 'G' greater the success in life.

Characteristics of S factor

1 It is learnt and hence acquired in the environment.

2 It varies from activity to activity in the same person.

3 The amount of 'S' also differs from person to person due to its accessibility to learning situations.

4 'S' factors are related to specific activity, a person can be expert

only in one or two activities because of the specific factor involved in the activity.

To spearman G factor is more important and thus it is an important measure of Intelligence. So any intelligence test should measure only the 'G' factor because it provides the most important basis for predicting a person's behaviour in different situations.

Raven's progressive matrices test and Cattel's culture fair test both measure G factor.

Spearman developed his two factor Theory of Intelligence using factor analysis.

Multi Factor Theory of Intelligence By E.L.Thorndike

E.L.Thorndike opposed the theory of General Intelligence by saying there are specific stimuli and specific responses. Intelligence is nothing more than a potential specific connection between stimuli and response. Differences in people are due to different numbers of such connections in the neurological system.

Attributes of Intelligence according to Thorndike there are four types of attributes of Intelligence according to Thorndike:

1 level: it refers to the difficulty of a task that can be removed by using intelligence. If different tasks are arranged in increasing difficulty order then the height that a person reaches determines his level of Intelligence.

Range: It refers to the number of tasks of the same difficulty value that a person can do in a certain period of time.

Area: It refers to the total number of situations at each level to which an individual is able to respond. Arae=level x range

Speed: refers to rapidly with which an individual can respond to a test item.

According to Thorndike every intelligence test should contain these four items.

Group Factor Theory by L.L.Thurstone (1938)

This theory was developed by L.L. thurstone. According to him intelligence is not an expression of general factors but a combination of a group of traits.

They are intermediate factors not as general as 'G' nor as specific as 'S' factor.

These primary groups of factors gives common mental abilities a functional cohesiveness and then constitute a group.

Thurstone identified following seven group factors which he termed as primary mental abilities:

Number factor: It is the ability to do numerical calculations rapidly and accurately.

Verbal factor: They are related to operations involving verbal comprehension.

Spatial Factor: it is related to the task in which the subject manipulates an object imaginary in space.

Word fluency factor: It is involved in the situation when the subject is asked to think of isolated words at a faster rate.

Reasoning factor: It is used in those tasks that require the subject to discover a rule or principle involved in a series or group of letters.

Rote memory: It is the ability to memorize a fact.

Perceptual factor: It is the ability to note visual details rapidly.

Assessment of Intelligence

We can observe the intelligence of an individual, only to the extent that it is manifested by him or her in one or more intelligence tests. Many such tests have been devised by psychologists for the measurement of Intelligence. In reference to these, however, the term assessment is preferred because, intelligence being only a concept or an abstraction rather than a substance, it cannot be measured in physical units like a length of cloth or temperature of the body.

In this context Griffith (1933) observes: "the standard of measurement is a group performance". Therefore when we measure an individual's intelligence by means of an intelligence test, we try to interpret his score in terms of the norm set (group performance) by the author of the test. One's intelligence is thus determined in relation to the classified group to which one belongs. Thus whereas a piece of cloth may be measured in absolute terms, relative measurement or assessment has to be resorted in the case of Intelligence.

classification of intelligence tests:

Intelligence tests may be classified broadly as follows:

1 individual tests: in which only one individual is tested at a time.

2 Group tests: is in which a group of individuals is tested at the same time.

Intelligence tests may also be classified on the basis of their form as verbal or language tests and nonverbal or non language tests.

Verbal or language tests: In this the subject makes use of language in which the instructions are given in words written or oral or both. The individuals being tested are required to use language, verbal or written for their responses.The test content is loaded with verbal material which may include varieties of the items including vocabulary test, memory test, comprehension test, information test, reasoning test and association test.

Non verbal and non language tests: These tests involve activities in which the use of language is not necessary, except for giving directions. Performance tests are a typical example of such tests.The main features of these are:

1 The content of the tests are in the form of material objects.

2 What is required of the subject is conveyed by the The tester

through oral instructions or by pantomium and signs.

3 The subject's responses are accepted in terms of how he reacts or what he does, rather than what he says or writes.

4 Generally these are individual tests.

Simon—Binet Scale (Verbal Test)

The Binet—Simon scale was created by the French psychologist Alfred Binet and his student Theodore Simon. Due to changing

education laws of the time, Binet had been requested by a government Commission to come up with a way to detect children who were falling behind developmentally and in need of help. 2 Binet believed that intelligence is malleable and that intelligence tests would help target children in need of extra attention to advance their intelligence.

3. To create their test Binet and Simon first created a baseline of Intelligence. A wide range of children were tested on a broad spectrum of measures in an effort to discover a clear indicator of Intelligence. Failing to find a single identifier of Intelligence, Binet and Simon instead   compared children in each category by age. The children's highest levels of achievements were sorted by age

and common levels of achievement considered the normal level for that age. Because this testing method merely compares a person's ability to the common ability level of others of their age, the general practices of the test can easily be transferred to test different populations even if the measures used are changed.

One of the first intelligence test is the Binet Simon test, quickly gained support in the psychological community many of whom further spread it to the public.Lewis M Terman a psychologist at Stanford university was one of the first to create a version of the test for the people in the United States naming the localised version the Stanford–binet intelligence scale. Terman used the test not only to help identify children with learning difficulties, but also to find children and adults who had above average levels of Intelligence in creating his version Terman also tested additional methods for his Stanford revision publishing his first official version as the measurement of Intelligence: an explanation of and a complete guide for the use of the Stanford revision an extension of the Binet–Simon intelligence scale. (Fancher and Rutherford 2012 Becker 2003)

The original tests in the 1905 form include:

1 "Le regard"

2 Pretensions provoked by a tactile stimulus

3 Pretensions provoked by a visual perception

4. Recognition of food

5 Quest of food complicated by a slight mechanical difficulty

6 Execution of simple commands and imitation of simple gestures

7 Verbal knowledge of object

8 Verbal knowledge of picture

9 Naming of designated objectives

10 Immediate comparison of two lines of unequal lengths

11 Repetition of three figures

12 Comparison of two weights

13 Suggestibility

14 Verbal definition of known objects

15 Repetition of sentences of 15 words

16 Comparisons of known objects from memory

17 Exercise of memory on pictures

18 Drawing a design from memory

19 Immediate repetition of figures

20 Resemblances of several known objects given from memory

21 Comparison of lengths

22 Five weights to be placed in order

23 Gap in weights

24 Exercise upon rhymes

25 Verbal Gaps to be filled

26 Synthesis of three words in one sentence

27 Reply to an abstract question

28 Reversal of the hands of a clock

29 Paper cutting

30 Definitions of abstract terms

Cattell Culture Fair Intelligence Test

The Culture Fair Intelligence Test (CFIT) was created by Raymond Cattell in 1949 as an attempt to measure cognitive abilities devoid of sociocultural and environmental influences. Scholars have subsequently concluded that the attempt to construct measures of cognitive abilities devoid of the influences of experiential and cultural conditioning is a challenging one. Cattell proposed that general intelligence (g) comprises both fluid intelligence (Gf) and crystallized intelligence (Gc). Whereas Gf is biologically and constitutionally based, Gc is the actual level of a person's cognitive functioning, based on the augmentation of Gf through sociocultural and experiential learning (including formal schooling).

The most widely used individual tests of cognitive abilities, such as the current editions of the Wechsler Adult Intelligence Scale and the Stanford–Binet Intelligence Scale, report cognitive ability scores as "deviation IQs" with 15 IQ points corresponding to one standard deviation above or below the mean, Cattell built into the CFIT a standard deviation of 24 IQ points.

Contents

Culture and age difference

Question Items

Culture and age difference

Crystallized intelligence (Gc) refers to that aspect of cognition in which initial intelligent judgments have become crystallized as habits. Fluid intelligence (Gf) is in several ways more fundamental and is particularly evident in tests requiring responses to novel situations. Before biological maturity individual differences between Gf and Gc will be mainly a function of differences in cultural opportunity and interest. Among adults, however, these discrepancies will also reflect differences with increasing age because the gap between Gc and Gf will tend to increase with experience which raises Gc, whereas Gf gradually declines as a result of declining brain function.

Question items

The Culture Fair tests consist of three scales with non-verbal visual puzzles. Scale I includes eight subtests of mazes, copying symbols, identifying similar drawings and other non-verbal tasks. Both Scales II and III consist of four subtests that include completing a sequence of drawings, a classification subtest where respondents pick a drawing that is different from other drawings, a matrix subtest that involves completing a matrix of patterns, and a conditions subtest which involves which, out of several geometric designs, fulfills a specific given condition.

Bhatia's Battery Test

Introduction

Bhatia's Battery of Performance Test of Intelligence was constructed by C. M. Bhatia in 1955. This test was developed to test the Intelligence of the Indian Population. It includes following five sub tests:

(i) Koh's Block Design Test: This battery includes 10 designs from the original 17 designs from the Koh's test. The time for the first five designs is 2 minutes and for the remaining five the time is 3 minutes. The cards with a variety of colored designs are shown to the test taker and he is asked to reproduce them using a set of colored blocks. Performance is based not just on the accuracy of the drawings but also on the examiner's observation of behaviour during the test, including such factors as attention level, self criticism and adaptive behaviour (such as self-help, communication, and social skills).

(ii) Alexander Pass-along Test: All the designs of the original test are included in this battery. The first four of these have to be completed in two minutes and the rest of the four have to be completed in 3 minutes.

(iii)Pattern Drawing Test: this test is constructed by Bhatia. This test includes eight cards. Every card has a pattern and the subject is required to draw these patterns in one go without lifting the pencil. The time for the first four cards is 2 minutes and for the rest of the four cards it is 3 minutes.

(iv) Immediate Memory: This test has two parts: digit span forward and digit span backward. The test taker is required to repeat the numbers the examiner says. The number of digits is increased on every trail. The test is continued till the subject repeats it successfully in the same order. This is a digit span forward. In the backward recall, the numbers are repeated in the backward position, from the last to the first. This recall is also continued till the subject successfully repeats the sequence.

(v) Picture Construction Test: This test requires the subject to construct a picture that is given in parts. The parts are to be meaningfully combined to construct the picture. The time for the first two pictures is 2 minutes and the rest of the three pictures it is

3 minutes.

Individual administration of this test takes less than one hour. Maximum 95 marks can be obtained in the complete test. Maximum marks for the 1st, 2nd, 3rd, 4th, and 5th test are 25, 20, 20, 15, 15 respectively. The main objective of the test is to measure the intelligence of children and less educated or illiterate Indians.

Glossary of terms:

Intelligence: The ability to understand and adapt to the environment by using inherited abilities and learned knowledge.

G Factor: The ability to reason and solve problems, or general intelligence.

S Factor: The ability to excel in certain areas or specific intelligence.

Intelligence Quotient: A number representing a measure of intelligence, resulting from the division of one's mental age by one's chronological age and then multiplying the quotient by 100.

Mental age: The level of native mental ability or capacity of an individual, usually as determined by intelligence test, in relation to the chronological age of the average individual at this level.

UNIT III

PERSONALITY

PERSONALITY

Uniqueness and consistency in the behaviour of individuals

Personality— an individual's unique and relatively stable patterns of behaviour, thoughts and emotions. (e.g., Nelson and Miller, 1995; Zuckerman 1995) or, as Friedman and Schustack (1999) have recently put it, "the psychological forces that make people unique". Personality should not be confused with character, which refers to value judgements made about a person's morals, or ethical behaviour should not be confused with temperament, the biologically innate and enduring characteristics with which each person is born, such as irritability or adaptability. Both character and temperament are vital parts of personality, however every adult personality is a combination of temperaments and personal history of family , culture and the time during which they grow up.

Personality: Is It Real?

Interest in personality is as old as civilization. Ancient philosophers and poets often speculated about why individuals were unique and why they differed from each other in so many ways. People have relied on the discipline of Astrology Palmistry, Tarot Cards, among others to get insights into themselves and significant others. It can be said that classification has been and continues to be a common urge among humans. There has been a strong tradition of typological theories since antiquity. For instance Charaka the father of Indian medicine in his compendium Charaka Sumhita gave humoural classification of personality (Prakriti) during 200 BC (Gopinath 2001). These humours were wind (Vatta) bile (Pita) And phlegm(Kapha) which constitute Tridosha Prakriti. Also, there exists a strong tradition of conceptualizing personality. It was not until the emergence of a scientific field of psychology, however that personality became the focus of systematic research. Yet although the study of personality now has a long history in psychology, it is important to note that there has been a continuing debate among psychologists about whether personality is actually real—whether individuals show enough consistency in their behaviour over time and across situations to make studying personality worthwhile. On one side of this issue, Walter Mischel (1985) argued that people show so much variability across situations that we cannot make any useful prediction about their behaviour from personality. Moreover he noted various traits generally show only modest correlation with over behaviour(0.20+0. 30).

In reply to such criticism other psychologists called attention to a growing body of evidence suggesting that in fact people do show a considerable degree of consistency, in their behaviour across situations—more than Mischel suggested for example (e.g.Steel at Ransch 1997) further, even when an individual shows contrasting patterns of behaviour in different situations, these actions may be functionally equivalent for that person in other words the behaviour may have the same meaning for the individual. For instance consider a woman who is very kindhearted in most situations and she gives help to others whenever they request it. In some cases though, she refuses. Why? Not because she no longer has an underlying and lasting tendency to be kind, but because she firmly believes that it is better in the long run for the person in question if she refuses. In other words, from her point of view this contrasting behaviour (saying yes and saying no to requests for help) actually serves the same purpose: assisting the people in question. Finally researchers who believe that personality is well worth studying note that correlation of 0.20 to 0.30 between aspects of personality and behaviour can be quite useful and are just as high as correlation between almost any factors and behaviour. (Friedman and Schustack 1999). Indeed, correlations much lower than 0.20 to 0.30 are often viewed as quite important—for instance the correlation between the amount of carbon dioxide in the earth's atmosphere and increase in temperature(the greenhouse effect).

Weighing all these points in the balance, most psychologists have reached the conclusion that personality is indeed real and worth studying. Indeed even Mischel, perhaps the arch–critic of studying personality, has focused on what he terms personal styles or strategies—individual differences in the meanings people assign to various situations and events(e.g.,Mischel and Shoda 1995). According to Miscel, individuals show considerable consistency in this respect, and such consistency in turn becomes a kind of behavioural signature of their personalities.

In short, our behaviour in any given situation is usually a complex function of both our personality(stable internal factors that make us unique individuals) and situational factors in the world around us. This interactionist perspective is the one currently accepted by most psychologists.[reference Robert barron]

Definitions of Personality

Watson (1930)

Personality is the sum of activities that can be discovered by actual observation over a long enough period of time to give reliable information.

Morton Prince (1929)

Personality is the sum total of all the biological innate dispositions, impulses, tendencies, appetites and instincts of the individual and the dispositions and tendencies acquired by experience.

Cattell (1970)

Personality is that which permits a prediction of what a person will do in a given situation.

Eysenck (1971)

Personality is the more or less stable and enduring organisation of a person's character,temperament, intellect and physique, which determine his unique adjustment to the environment.

S R Maddi (1976)

Personality is the stable set of characteristics and tendencies that determine those commonalities and differences in the psychological behaviour(thoughts, feelings and actions) of people that have continuity in time and that may or may not be easily understood in terms of the social and biological pressures of the immediate situation alone.

Allport (1948)

Personality is a dynamic organisation within the individual of those psychophysical systems that determine his unique adjustment to his environment.

According to K. Young,

"Personality is a patterned body of habits, traits, attitudes and ideas of an individual's, as these are organised externally into roles and statues and as they relate internally to motivation, goals, and various aspects of selfhood.

Ogburn

Personality means "the integration of the socio-psychological behaviour of the human being, represented by habits of action and feeling, attitudes and opinions."

Lundberg and others,

"The term personality refers to the habits, attitudes and other social traits that are characteristic of a given individual's behaviour".

Lawrence A. Pewin

"Personality represents those structural and dynamic properties of an individual or individuals as they reflect themselves in characteristic responses to situations". This is the working definition of personality.

Characteristics of Personality:

1. Personality is something which is unique in each individual:

Personality refers to internal as well as external qualities, some of which are quite general. But it is unique to each individual. It is not possible for any other individual to reproduce or imitate the qualities of the personality of the individual.

2. Personality refers particularly to persistent qualities of an individual:

Every individual has certain feelings as well as other permanent traits and qualities. Personality is mainly composed of the persistent or permanent qualities that exhibit themselves in the form of social behaviour and attempt to make adjustments with the environment.

3. Personality represents a dynamic orientation of organism to environment:

Personality represents the process of learning. It takes place in reference to the environment. We do not acquire all the traits of personality all at once.

4. Personality is greatly influenced by social interactions:

Personality is not an individual quality. It is a result of social-interaction. In other words, it means that when we come in contact with other members of the society, we acquire certain qualities while we exhibit certain others. All these come to form personality.

5. Personality represents a unique organisation of persistent dynamic and social predisposition:

In personality various qualities are not put together. They are, in fact, integrated into one. This integration is nothing but a result of organisation which may be different from man to man. The behaviour of a person directed to one particular individual may differ from the behaviour of another person. That is why; we put the condition of a suitable environment. This suitability is concerned with individual specificity.

Theories of Personality:

Type Theory:

In the 1940's, William Herbert Sheldon associated body types with human temperament types. He claimed that a body type could be linked with the personality of that person. He says that a fat person with a large bone structure tends to have an outgoing and more relaxed personality while a more muscular body type person is more active and aggressive. A slim or scrawny person with thin muscles is usually characterized as quiet or fragile. He split up these body/personality types into three categories called somatotypes.

Endomorph

An Endomorphic somatotype is also known as a viscerotonic. The characteristic traits of this somatotype usually includes being relaxed, tolerant, comfortable, and sociable. Psychologically, they are also fun loving, good humoured ,even tempered, and they love food and affection. The Endomorph is physically "round". They have wide hips and narrow shoulders that give a pear shape. They tend to have a lot of extra fat on their body and on their arms and thighs. They have skinny ankles and wrists that make the rest of their body look even bigger. The Endomorph is physically quite 'round', and is typified as the 'barrel of fun' person.

They tend to have:

Wide hips and narrow shoulders, which makes them rather pear shaped.

Quite a lot of fat spread across the body, including upper arms and thighs.

They have quite slim ankles and wrists, which only serves to accentuate the fatter other parts.

Psychologically, the endomorph is:

Sociable

Fun loving

Love of food

Tolerant

Even Tempered

Good humored

Relaxed

With a love of comfort

And has a need for affection

Ectomorph

An ectomorph is the complete opposite of the Endomorph. Physically, they have narrow shoulders, thin legs and arms, little fat on the body, a narrow face and a narrow chest. They may eat just as much as the endomorph but never seem to gain any weight. They always stay skinny. Personality wise, they tend to be self-conscious, socially anxious, artistic, thoughtful, quiet, and private. They always keep to themselves and are afraid to branch out.

Physically, they tend to have:

Narrow shoulders and hips

A thin and narrow face, with a high forehead

A thin and narrow chest and abdomen

Thin legs and arms

Very little body fat

Even though they may eat as much as the endomorph, they never seem to put on weight (much to the endomorph's chagrin).

Psychologically they are:

Self Conscious

Private

Introverted

Inhibited

Socially anxious

Artistic

Intense

Emotionally restrained

Thoughtful

Mesomorphic

The mesomorph is in between the endomorph and thin ectomorph. They have an attractive and desirable body. Physically, they tend to have a large head and broad shoulders with a narrow waist.

They have a strong muscular body and strong arms and legs and little fat on the body. They work

for the body they have so that they could have an attractive body.Psychologically, the mesomorph is adventurous and courageous. They are not afraid to break out and do new things with new people. They are assertive and competitive and have a desire to have power and be dominant. They love taking risks and chances in life. The mesomorph is somewhere between the round endomorph and the thin ectomorph.

Physically, they have the more 'desirable' body, and have:

Large head, broad shoulders and narrow waist (wedge shaped).

Muscular body, with strong forearms and and thighs

Very little body fat

They are generally considered as 'well proportioned'.

Psychologically, they are:

Adventurous

Courageous

Indifferent to what others think or want

Assertive/bold

Zest for physical activity

Competitive

With a desire for power/dominance

And a love of risk/chance

Is This True?

Profiling psychologically based on physical features is very unreliable but these observations tend to be true. These patterns are noticed by society. Most of society would agree with these observations made by Sheldon.

The best approach is to use this as a test. When you meet a person who seems to fit in with the physical characteristics above, be curious to see if they also fit into the psychological profile. If it all works as predicted, then well and good (it may be that they are actually in a self-fulfilling prophecy, where they fit themselves to the appropriate model). Otherwise, look elsewhere for ways to understand the person.

Sheldon's original work included attempts to characterize criminals (in the style of Lombroso's original work in this area). Unsurprisingly, he found that a number were muscular mesomorphs, as violent crimes are likely to be carried out by strong men. The trap beyond this is to assume that all mesomorphs are criminal in nature

Sheldon's Somatotype	Character	Shape	Sample Picture
Endomorph [viscerotonic]	relaxed, sociable, tolerant, comfort-loving, peaceful	plump, buxom, developed visceral structure	
Mesomorph [somatotonic]	active, assertive, vigorous, combative	muscular	
Ectomorph [cerebrotonic	quiet, fragile, restrained, non-assertive, sensitive	lean, delicate, poor muscles	

Jung: The Collective Unconscious

Perhaps the most bitter of all the defections Freud had experienced was that of Carl Jung—the following Freud viewed as his heir apparent. Jung shared Freud's views concerning the importance of the unconscious, but contended that there is another part to this aspect of personality that Freud overlooked: the collective unconscious. According to Jung, the collective unconscious holds experiences shared by all human beings—experiences that are, in a sense, part of or biological heritage. The contents of the collective unconscious, in short, reflect the experiences our species has had since it originated on earth. The collective unconscious finds expression in our minds in several ways, but among these archetypes are the most central to Jung's theory. These are manifestations of the collective unconscious

that express themselves when our conscious mind is distracted or inactive; for example during sleep, in dreams or in fantasies (e.g., Nehar 1996). The specific expression of archetypes depends in part on our unique experience as individuals, but in all cases such images are representations of key aspects of the human experience—-mother, father, wise old man, the sun, the moon and the hero. It is because of these shared innate images, Jung contended, that the folklore of many different cultures contains similar figures and themes.

Two especially important archetypes in Jung's theory are known as animus and anima. The animus is the masculine side of females, while the anima is the feminine side of males. Jung believed that in looking for a mate, we search for the person on whom we can best project these hidden sides of our personality. When there is a good match between such projections and another person attraction occurs.

Another aspect of Jung's theory was his suggestion that we are all born with innate tendencies to be concerned primarily either with our inner selves or with the outside world. Jung labeled persons in the first category introverts and described them as being hesitant and cautious; introverts do not make friends easily and prefer to observe the world rather than become involved in it. He labeled persons in the second category extroverts. Such persons are open and confident, make friends readily, and enjoy high levels of stimulation and a wide range of activities. Although many aspects of Jung's theory have been rejected by psychologists—-especially the idea of the collective unconscious—the dimensions of introversion–extroversion appears to be a basic one of major importance; it is included in several trait theories also. (reference Robert barron]

Trait Theories:

Seeking the Key Dimensions of Personality

When we describe other persons, we often do so in terms of specific personality traits— stable dimensions of personality along which people vary, from very low to very high. This strong tendency to think about others in terms of specific characteristics is reflected in trait theories of personality. Such theories focus on identifying key dimensions of personality—--the most important ways in which people differ. The basic idea behind this approach is as follows: Once we identify the key dimensions along which people differ, we can measure how much they differ and can relate such differences to many important forms of behaviour.

Unfortunately, this task sounds easier than it actually is. Human beings differ in an almost countless number of ways. How can we determine which of these are most important and stable(i.e.,lasting). One approach is to search for clusters—-groups of traits that seem to go together. We will now take a brief look at a Theory that adopted this approach Allport's trait theory of personality.

Allport's trait theory of personality

The search for basic traits:

One of the first efforts to identify key human traits—the most important dimensions along which personalities vary—-was the work of Gordon Allport. He proposed that personality traits could be divided into several categories that varied in their importance.

The least important are secondary traits: these are traits that exert relatively weak and limited effects on behaviour. More important are Central traits—5 to 10 traits that together account for the uniqueness of an individual's personality. Such traits are stronger and more resistant to situational forces. Finally Allport noted that a few people are dominated by a single all important Cardinal trait. A few examples of such persons and the Cardinal traits that seemed to drive their personalities: Napoleon (ambition) Florence Nightingale (empathy) Alexander the Great (lust for power) Don Jon (just plain lust).

Perhaps an even more important aspect of Allport's theory of personality is his concept of functional autonomy(Allport 1965)--- the idea that patterns of behaviour that are initially acquired under one set of circumstances, and which satisfy one set of motives,may later be performed for very different reasons. For example initially a child may learn to read because this pleases his teachers and parents and because failure to do so is punished. Later in life however, the same person may read because he has come to enjoy this activity in and of itself—it is in terms of our discussion on Intrinsic motivation. Notice how this contrasts with Freud's view that the roots of adult personality are planted firmly in the soil of childhood—-that, as Freud put it "The child is the father (mother) of the man (women)". For Allport such connections are not necessarily present, and our adult behaviour may spring from roots entirely different from those that give rise to our childhood behaviour. [Reference Robert barron]

Cattell's Theory:

Another and in some ways more sophisticated trait theory was proposed by Raymond Cattell. Two hundred traits is still a very large number of descriptors. How might an employer be able to judge the personality of a potential employee looking at a list of 200 traits? A more compact way of describing personality was needed. Raymond Cattell (1990) defined two types of traits as surface traits and source traits. Surface traits are like those found by Allport, representing the personality characteristics easily seen by other people. Source traits are those more basic traits that underlie the surface traits. For example, shyness, being quiet and disliking crowds might all be surface traits related to the more basic source trait of introversion, a tendency to withdraw from excessive stimulation.

Using a statistical technique that looks for groupings and commonalities in numerical data called factor analysis, Cattell identified 16 source traits (Cattell, 1950, 1966), and although he later determined that there might be another 7 source traits to make a total of 23 (Cattell & Kline, 1977), he developed, his assessment questionnaire, The Sixteen Personality factor (16PF) Questionnaire (Cattell, 1995), based on just 16 source traits. These 16 source traits are seen as trait dimensions, or continuums, in which there are two opposite traits at each end with a range of possible degrees for each trait measurable along the dimension. For example, someone scoring near the "reserved" end of the "reserved/outgoing dimension would be more introverted than someone scoring in the middle or at the opposite end.

MODERN TRAIT THEORIES: The "Big Five"

Identify the five trait dimensions of the five-factor model of personality.

By now, you may be running out of patience. "OK," we can almost hear you saying, "how many basic traits or dimensions of personality are there?" This is one time when we can offer you a fairly definite answer, because research conducted during the past twenty years has converged on the following conclusion: In fact, there may be only five key or central dimensions of personality (e.g., Costa & McCrae, 1994; Zuckerman, 1994). These are sometimes labeled the "big five, and they can be described with an acronym **OCEAN** 1 Openness, Conscientiousness, Extraversion, Agreeableness and Neuroticism (emotional stability).

Openness can best be described as a person's willingness to try new things and be open to new experiences. People who try to maintain the status quo and who don't like to change things would score low on openness.

Conscientiousness refers to a person's organization and motivation, with people who score high in this dimension being those who are careful about being placed on time and careful with belongings as well. Someone scoring low on this dimension, for example, might always be late to important social events or borrow belongings and fail to return them or return them in poor condition.

Extraversion is a term first used by Carl Jung (1933), who believed that all people could be divided into two personality types: extraverts and introverts. Extraverts are outgoing and sociable, whereas introverts are more solitary and dislike being the center of attention.

Agreeableness refers to the basic emotional style of a person, who may be easy going, friendly, and pleasant (at the high end of the scale) or grumpy, crabby, and hard to get along with (at the low end).

Neuroticism refers to emotional instability or stability. People who ate excessive worriers, overanxious, and moody would score high on this dimension, whereas calm would score low.

Sigmund Freud

The Psychoanalytic Approach

Freud's Theory of Personality

Freud entered private medical practice soon after graduation from Medical school. A turning point in his early career came when he won a research grant to travel to Paris to observe the work of Jean-Martin Charcot, Who was then using hypnosis to treat several types of mental disorders. When Freud returned to Vienna, he worked with Joseph Breuer, a colleague who was using hypnosis in the treatment of Hysteria—a condition in which individuals experienced physical symptoms such as blindness, deafness or paralysis of arms or legs for which there seemed to be no underlying physical cause. Out of these experiences and his growing clinical practice, Freud gradually developed his theories of human personality and mental illness. His ideas were Complex and touched on many different issues. With respect to personality, however, four topics are most central: levels of consciousness, the structure of personality, anxiety and defense mechanisms and psychosexual stages of development.

Levels of Consciousness: beneath the Iceberg's Tip

Freud viewed himself as a scientist, and applied to the task of understanding the human mind some of the emerging ideas about sensory thresholds and the possibility of responding to stimuli we cannot report perceiving. He soon reached the startling conclusion that most of the mind lies below the surface—-below the threshold of conscious experience. Above this boundary is the realm of the conscious. This includes our current thoughts; whatever we are thinking about or experiencing at a given moment. Beneath this conscious realm is the much larger preconscious. This contains memories that are not part of current thought but can readily be brought to mind if the need arises. Finally beneath the preconscious and forming the bulk of the human mind is the unconscious: thoughts, Desires and impulses of which we remain largely unaware. Although some of this material has always been unconscious. Freud believed that much of it was once conscious but has been actively repressed—-driven from consciousness because it was too anxiety provoking. For example, Freud contended that shameful experiences or unacceptable sexual or aggressive urges are often driven deep within the unconscious. The fact that we are not aware of them. However in no way prevents them from affecting our behaviour. Indeed Freud believed that many of the symptoms experienced by his patients were disguised and indirect reflections of repressed thoughts and desires. This is why one major goal of psychoanalysis—the method of treating psychological disorders devised by Freud—-is to bring repressed material back into consciousness. Presumably, once such material is made conscious and patients gain insight into the early life experiences that caused them to repress it in the first place, important causes of mental illness are removed.

Freud believes that one way of probing the unconscious was through the interpretation of Dreams. In dreams, Freud believed we can give expression to impulses and desires we find unacceptable during our waking hours. Unfortunately there is little scientific evidence for this view.

The Structure of Personality Id, Ego and Superego

Freud suggested that personality consists largely of three parts: the id, the ego and the superego as these correspond to desire, reason and conscience.

The **id** consists of all our primitive innate urges. These include various bodily needs, sexual Desire and aggressive impulses. According to Freud, the id is totally unconscious and operates in accordance with what he termed the pleasure principle: It demands immediate, total gratification and is not capable of considering the potential cost of seeking this goal.

Unfortunately the world offers few opportunities for instant pleasure. Moreover, attempting to gratify many of our innate urges would soon get us into serious trouble. It is in this response to these facts that the second structure of personality, the **ego**, develops. The ego's task is to hold the id in check until conditions allow for satisfaction of its impulses. Thus the ego operates in accordance with the reality principle: It takes into account external conditions and the consequences of various actions and directs behaviour so as to maximize pleasure and minimize pain. The ego is partly conscious but not entirely so; thus some of its actions—for example its eternal struggle with the id—are outside our conscious knowledge or understanding.

The final aspect of personality described by Freud is the **superego**. It too seeks to control satisfaction of impulses; but, in contrast to the ego it is concerned with morality—-with whether various ways that could potentially satisfy id impulses are right or wrong. The superego permits us to gratify such impulses only when it is morally correct to do so—not simply when it is safe or feasible as required by the ego.

The superego is acquired from our parents and through experience and represents our internalization of the moral teachings and norms of our society. Unfortunately, such teachings are often quite inflexible and leave little room for gratification of our basic desires—-they require us to be good all the time. Because of this fact, the ego faces another difficult task: it must strike a balance between our primitive urges (the id) and our learning moral constraints (the superego). Freud felt that this constant struggle among id, ego and superego plays a key role in personality and in many psychological disorders. Moreover he suggested that the struggle was often visible in everyday behaviour in what have come to be known as Freudian slips—errors in speech that actually reflect unconscious impulses that have "gotten by" the ego or superego. An example" she was tempting—I mean attempting to". According to Freud the word tempting reveals an unacceptable sexual Impulse.

Anxiety and Defense Mechanism: Self-Protection by the Ego

In its constant struggle to prevent the eruption of dangerous Id impulses, the ego faces a difficult task. Yet for most people, most of the time, the ego succeeds. Sometimes though, id impulses grow so strong that they threaten to get out of control. For example consider the case of a middle-aged widow who finds herself strongly attracted to her daughter's boyfriend. She hasn't had a romantic attachment in years, so her sexual desire quickly rises to high levels. What happens next? According to Freud, when her ego senses that unacceptable impulses are about to get out of hand, It experiences anxiety—intense feelings of nervousness, tension or worry. These feelings occur because the unacceptable impulses are getting closer and closer to consciousness, as well as closer and closer to the limits of the ego to hold them in check.

At this point Freud contended the ego may resort to one of several different defense mechanisms. These are all designed to keep unacceptable impulses from the id out of consciousness and to prevent their open expression. Defense mechanisms take many different forms. For example in sublimation, the unacceptable impulse is channeled into some socially acceptable action. Instead of trying to seduce the young man, as Freud would say the widow's id wants to do, she might "adopt" him as a son and provide financial support to further his education. Other defense mechanisms are Repression, Rationalization, Displacement Projection and Regression. These all function to reduce anxiety by keeping unacceptable urges and impulses from breaking into consciousness.

Psychosexual Stages of Development

Now we come to what is perhaps the most controversial aspect of Freud's theory of personality: his ideas about its formation or development. Freud's views in this respect can be grouped under the heading psychosexual stages of development: innately determined stages of sexual development through which, presumably, we all pass, and which strongly shape the nature of our personality. Before turning to the stages themselves, however, we must first consider two important concept related to them libido and fixation

Libido refers to the instinctual life force that energizes the id. Release of libido is closely related to pleasure, but the focus of such pleasure—and the expression of libido—changes as we develop. In each stage of development, we obtain different kinds of pleasure and leave behind a small amount of our libido—this is the normal course of events. If an excessive amount of libido energy is tied to a particular stage, however, fixation results. This can stem from either too little or too much gratification during this stage, and in either case the result is harmful. Because the individual has left too much "psychic energy" behind, less is available for full adult development. The outcome may be an adult personality reflecting the stage or stages at which fixation has occurred. To put it another way, if too much energy is drained away by fixation at an early stage of development, the amount remaining may be insufficient to power movement to full adult development. Then an individual may show an immature personality and several psychological disorders.

Now back to the actual stages themselves. According to Freud, as we grow and develop, different parts of the body serve as the focus of our quest for pleasure. In the initial **oral stage**, lasting until we are about 18 months old, we seek pleasure mainly through the mouth. If too much or too little gratification occurs during this stage, an individual may become fixated at it. Too little gratification results in a personality that is overly dependent on others; too much, especially after the child has developed some teeth, results in a personality that is excessively hostile, especially through verbal sarcasm.

The next stage occurs in response to efforts by parents to toilet train their children. During the **anal stage**, the process of elimination becomes the primary focus of pleasure. Fixation at this stage stemming from overly harsh toilet–training experiences may result in individuals who are excessively orderly or compulsive— they cannot leave any job unfinished and strive for perfection and neatness in everything they do. In contrast, fixation stemming from very relaxed toilet training may result in people who are undisciplined, impulsive and excessively generous. Freud himself might well be described as compulsive; even when he was seriously ill he personally answered dozens of letters everyday— even letters from total strangers asking his advice(Benjamin Dixon 1996).

At about age four the genitals become the primary source of pleasure, and children enter the **phallic stage**. Freud speculated that at this time we fantasize about sex with our opposite sex parent, a phenomenon he termed the Oedipus complex, after Oedipus a character in ancient Greek literature who unknowingly killed his father and then married his mother. Fear of punishment for such desires then enters the picture. Among boys the feared punishment is Castration, leading to Castration anxiety. Among girls the feared punishment is loss of love, in both cases these fears bring about resolution of the Oedipus complex and identification with the same–sex parent. In other words, little boys give up sexual desire for their mothers and come to see their father's models rather than as rivals; little girls give up their sexual desires for their father and come to see their mother as models.

Perhaps one of Freud's most controversial suggestions is the idea that little girls experience penis envy stemming from their own lack of a male organ. Freud suggested that because of such envy, girls experience strong feelings of inferiority and envy feelings they carry with them in disguised form even in adult life. As you can readily imagine, many psychologists object strongly to these ideas, and there is virtually no evidence for them.

After the resolution of the Oedipus complex conflict, children enter the **latency stage**, during which sexual urges are according to Freud at a minimum. Finally, during puberty adolescents enter the **genital stage**. During this stage pleasure is again focused on the genitals. Now, however, lust is blended with affection, and people become capable of adult love. Remember, according to Freud, progression to this final stage is possible only if serious fixation has not occurred at the earliest stages. If such fixation exists development is blocked and various disorders result. [reference Robert barron]

Assessment of personality:

The Minnesota Multiphasic Personality Inventory (MMPI) is the most widely used and researched clinical assessment tool used by mental health professionals to help diagnose mental health disorders.

Originally developed in the late 1930s, the test has been revised and updated several times to improve accuracy and validity. The MMPI-2 consists of 567 true-false questions and takes approximately 60 to 90 minutes to complete; the MMPI-2-RF has 338 true-false questions, taking 35 to 50 minutes to finish.

This article discusses how the MMPI was developed, how it is used, and the different versions of the instrument that are available.

History of the MMPI

The Minnesota Multiphase Personality Inventory (MMPI) was developed in 1937 by clinical psychologist Starke R. Hathaway and neuropsychiatric J. Charnley McKinley at the University of Minnesota. They originally developed the test to be used in the Department of Psychology at the University of Minnesota. The goal was to develop an instrument that could be used as an objective tool for assessing different psychiatric conditions and their severity.

The creators of the test felt that the self-report inventories of the time were too transparent. Because respondents could easily guess the intent of these inventories, they could also manipulate the results with ease.

Test items were originally developed by selecting questions that have been endorsed by people diagnosed with different mental health conditions.

The test grew to become one of the most widely used psychological assessments. It was utilized in psychology clinics, hospitals, correctional facilities, and pre-employment screenings.

Today, it's the most frequently used clinical testing instrument and is one of the most researched psychological tests in existence. While the MMPI is not a perfect test, it remains a valuable tool in the diagnosis and treatment of mental illness.

How the Test Has Changed

In the years after the test was first published, clinicians and researchers began to question the accuracy of the MMPI. Critics pointed out that the original sample group was inadequate. Others argued that the results indicated possible test bias, while others felt the test itself contained sexist and racist questions.

In response to these issues, the MMPI underwent a revision in the late 1980s. Many questions were removed or reworded while a number of new questions were added. Additionally, new validity scales were incorporated in the revised test.

MMPI-2: The revised edition of the test was released in 1989 as the MMPI-2.The test received revision again in 2001 and updates in 2003 and 2009, and it's still in use today as the most frequently used clinical assessment test.

MMPI-2-RF: Another edition of the test, published in 2008, is known as the Minnesota Multiphasic Personality Inventory-2-Restructured Form (MMPI-2-RF), an alternative to the MMPI-2.

MMPI-A: There is also an MMPI, published in 1992, that's geared toward adolescents aged 14 to 18 years old called the MMPI-A. With 478 questions, it takes about an hour to complete.

MMPI-A-RF: In 2016, the Minnesota Multiphase Personality Inventory-Adolescent-Restructured Form (MMPI-A-RF) was published. Like the MMPI-2-RF, it's shorter, with just 241 questions that take 25 to 45 minutes to answer.

MMPI-3: The latest version of the instrument, MMPI-3, was released in 2020. The test takes 25 to 50 minutes to complete and is available in English, Spanish, and French for Canada formats.7

How the MMPI Is Used

The MMPI is most commonly used by mental health professionals to assess and diagnose mental illness, but it has also been utilized in other fields outside of clinical psychology. The MMPI-2 is often used in legal cases, including criminal defense and custody disputes.

The test has also been used as a screening instrument for certain professions, especially high-risk jobs, although using it in this manner has been controversial. It's also used to evaluate the effectiveness of treatment programs, including substance use programs.

Administration

The MMPI-2 contains 567 test items and takes approximately 60 to 90 minutes to complete. The MMPI-2-RF contains 338 questions and takes around 35 to 50 minutes to finish. The MMPI-3 contains 335 self-report items and takes 25 to 35 minutes to administer by computer and 35 to 40 minutes to administer by paper and pencil.

Additionally, the MMPI is copyrighted by the University of Minnesota, which means clinicians must pay to administer and utilize the test.

The MMPI should be administered, scored, and interpreted by a professional, preferably a clinical psychologist or psychiatrist, who has received special training in MMPI use.

The MMPI test should be used with other assessment tools as well. A diagnosis should never be made solely on the results of the MMPI.

The MMPI can be administered individually or in groups and computerized versions are available as well. Both the MMPI-2 and the MMPI-2-RF are designed for individuals aged 18 years and older.

The test can be scored by hand or by a computer, but the results should always be interpreted by a qualified mental health professional that has had extensive training in MMPI interpretation.

10 Clinical Scales

The MMPI-2 and MMPI-A have 10 clinical scales that are used to indicate different psychological conditions, though the MMPI-2-RF and the MMPI-A-RF use different scales.9

Despite the names given to each scale, they are not a pure measure since many conditions have overlapping symptoms. Because of this, most psychologists simply refer to each scale by number.

Here's a brief overview of the clinical scales on the MMPI-2 and the MMPI-A.9

Scale 1—**Hypochondriasis**

This scale was designed to assess a neurotic concern over bodily functioning. The items on this scale concern physical symptoms and well-being. It was originally developed to identify people displaying the symptoms of hypochondria, or a tendency to believe that one has an undiagnosed medical condition.

Scale 2—**Depression**

This scale was originally designed to identify depression, characterized by poor morale, lack of hope in the future, and general dissatisfaction with one's own life situation. Very high scores may indicate depression, while moderate scores tend to reveal a general dissatisfaction with one's life.

Scale 3—**Hysteria**

The third scale was originally designed to identify those who display hysteria or physical complaints in stressful situations. Those who are well-educated and of a high social class tend to score higher on this scale. Women also tend to score higher than men on this scale.

Scale 4—**Psychopathic Deviate**

Originally developed to identify psychopathic individuals, this scale measures social deviation, lack of acceptance of authority, and amorality (a disregard for morality). This scale can be thought of as a measure of disobedience and antisocial behaviour.

High scorers tend to be more rebellious, while low scorers are more accepting of authority. Despite the name of this scale, high scorers are usually diagnosed with a personality disorder rather than a psychotic disorder.

Scale 5—**Masculinity-Femininity**

This scale was designed by the original authors to identify what they referred to as "homosexual tendencies," for which it was largely ineffective. Today, it is used to assess how much or how little a person identifies how rigidly an individual identifies with stereotypical male and female gender roles.

Scale 6—Paranoia

This scale was originally developed to identify individuals with paranoid symptoms such as suspiciousness, feelings of persecution, grandiose self-concepts, excessive sensitivity, and rigid attitudes. Those who score high on this scale tend to have paranoid or psychotic symptoms.

Scale 7—Psychasthenia

This diagnostic label is no longer used today and the symptoms described on this scale are more reflective of anxiety, depression, and obsessive-compulsive disorder. This scale was originally used to measure excessive doubts, compulsions, obsessions, and unreasonable fears.

Scale 8—Schizophrenia

This scale was originally developed to identify individuals with schizophrenia. It reflects a wide variety of areas including bizarre thought processes and peculiar perceptions, social alienation, poor familial relationships, difficulties in concentration and impulse control, lack of deep interests, disturbing questions of self-worth and self-identity, and sexual difficulties.

The scale can also show potential substance abuse, emotional or social alienation, eccentricities, and a limited interest in other people.

Scale 9—**Hypomania**

This scale was developed to identify characteristics of hypomania such as elevated mood, hallucinations, delusions of grandeur, accelerated speech and motor activity, irritability, flight of ideas, and brief periods of depression.

Scale 10—**Social Introversion**

This scale was developed later than the other nine scales. It's designed to assess a person's shyness and tendency to withdraw from social contacts and responsibilities.

Validity Scales

All of the MMPI tests use validity scales of varying sorts to help assess the accuracy of each individual's answers. Since these tests can be used for circumstances like employment screenings and custody hearings, test takers may not be completely honest in their answers.

Validity scales can show how accurate the test is, as well as to what degree answers may have been distorted. The MMPI-2 uses the following scales.

The L Scale

Also referred to as the lie scale, this "uncommon virtues" validity scale was developed to detect attempts by individuals to present themselves in a favorable light.

People who score high on this scale deliberately try to present themselves in the most positive way possible, rejecting shortcomings or unfavorable characteristics.

The F Scale

This scale is used to detect attempts at over reporting. Essentially, people who score high on this scale are trying to appear worse than they really are, they may be in severe psychological distress, or they may be just randomly answering questions without paying attention to what the questions say.

This scale asks questions designed to determine if test-takers are contradicting themselves in their responses.

The K Scale

Sometimes referred to as the "defensiveness scale," this scale is a more effective and less obvious way of detecting attempts to present oneself in the best possible way by underreporting.

People may underreport because they're worried about being judged or they may be minimizing their problems or denying that they have any problems at all.

The ? Scale

Also known as the "cannot say" scale, this validity scale assesses the number of items left unanswered. The MMPI manual recommends that any test with 30 or more unanswered questions should be declared invalid.

TRIN Scale

The True Response Inconsistency (TRIN) scale was developed to detect people who use fixed responding, a method of taking the test without regard to the question, such as marking ten questions "true," the next ten as "false," and so on.

Fixed responding could be used due to not being able to read or comprehend the test material well or being defiant about having to take the test. This section consists of 20 paired questions that are the opposite of each other.

VRIN Scale

The Variable Response Inconsistency (VRIN) scale is another method developed to detect inconsistent, random responses. Like fixed responding, this can be intentional or it can be due to not understanding the material or not being able to read it.

The Fb Scale

This scale is designed to show changes in how a person responded in the first half of the test versus how they responded in the second half by using questions that most normal respondents didn't support.

High scores on this scale sometimes indicate that the respondent stopped paying attention and began answering questions randomly. It can also be due to over or underreporting, fixed responding, becoming tired, or being under severe stress.

The Fp Scale

This scale helps detect intentional over reporting in people who have a mental health disorder of some sort or who were using random or fixed responding.

The FBS Scale

The "symptom validity" scale is used for people who are taking the test because they're claiming that they had a personal injury or disability. This scale can help establish the credibility of the test taker.

The S Scale

The "superlative self-presentation" scale was developed in 1995 to look for additional underreporting. It also has sub-scales that assess the test taker's belief in human goodness, serenity, contentment with life, patience/denial of irritability, and denial of moral flaws

[reference verywell mind]

16 PF

Another example of a pencil paper test is the 16 personality factor questionnaire.The sixteen Personality Factor (16 PF) questionnaire was first developed by Raymond Catell in the 1940s. It is a test that measures the 16 basic personality traits in standard Ten (Sten) scores. Some of the 16 basic personality factors like warmth, intelligence, emotional stability, dominance, surgency, amiability, sensibility, abstractedness, artistic ability, assertiveness, self-stuffiness, radicalism etc.

The 16 Pf -Form A has 187 questions. Each question has three alternative answers. A separate answer sheet is provided for the subject to mark her answers. Although it is a self-administered personality test, the final calculation and interpretation is done by the test taker.

The test measures once the answer sheet is marked, with the help of a scoring key the test taker calculates the scores which are called the raw scores. These raw scores are then converted to Sten scores are then marked in the 16 PF Test Profile sheet. In this sheet, the marked dots can be connected to sketch a graphical representation of the Standard Ten Score.

The Sten scores of 1, 2 and 3 are considered low and 8, 9 and 10 are considered high. These scores are used to interpret the subject's profile and therefore these personality factors are important in recognizing her personality traits. The scores from 4 to 7 are considered average.

The manual (in #3 above) comprises orientation to the 16 PF test, the design and construction, instruction, principles and mechanisms of scoring, converting raw scores to Sten scores, interpretation of the primary factors, brief descriptions of all the 16 personality factors, second order scores calculating procedures, followed by the bibliography.

The second manual (material # 4 also consists of a brief orientation followed 16 d by norm tables which are further classified to male and female groups of various.

These are the primary source traits covered by the 16 PF Test:

Factor A warmth -A person obtaining low Sten score (1-3) is considered to be cool, reserved, distant, impersonal, Schizothymia and a person obtaining high Sten score (8-10) is considered warm, outgoing, easy going participating attentive to others, Affeclothymia, formerly cyclothymia.

Factor B: Reasoning – A person obtaining a low Sten score (1-3) is considered to have a lower mental capacity and concrete thinking, whereas a person obtaining a high Sten score (8-10) is considered to be intelligent, bright, fast-learner.

Factor C: Emotional Stability – A person obtaining low score (1-3) is considered to be easily affected by feelings, easily annoyed, and has lower ego strength; whereas, a person obtaining high Sten score (8-10) is considered to be mature, emotionally stable, calm etc.

Factor E: Dominance – A person obtaining low Sten score (1-3) is considered to be co-operative, accommodating, submissive, whereas, a person obtaining high Sten score (8-10) is considered to be dominant, bossy, competitive, forceful, stubborn, Dominance.

Factor F: Liveliness – A person obtaining a low score (1-3) is considered to be serious, sober, restrained, careful, desurgency; whereas, a person obtaining a high Sten score (8-10) is considered to be enthusiastic, cheerful, spontaneous, surreptitious.

Factor G: Rule Consciousness – A person obtaining a low Sten score (1-3) is considered to be expedient, non-confirming, weaker superego strength, whereas a person obtaining a high score (8-10) is conscientious, dutiful, rule-bound etc.

Factor H: Social boldness- A person obtaining low Sten score (1-3) is considered to be shy, hesitant, intimidated, Threptic, whereas a person obtaining high score (8-10) is considered to be bold, venturesome, uninhibited.

Factor I: Sensitivity -A person obtaining low Sten score (1-3) is considered to be tough minded, realistic, objective, Harria; whereas a person obtaining high score (8-10) is considered to be tender-minded, sensitive Premsia.

Factor L: Vigilance – A person obtaining low Sten score (1-3) is considered to be, trusting, accepting unsuspecting, Alaxia; whereas a person obtaining high score (8-10) is considered to be wary, skeptical, suspicious, Protension.

Factor M: Abstractedness – A person obtaining low Sten score (1-3) is considered to be practical grounded, down to earth, Praxemia expedient, whereas a person obtaining high score (8-10) is considered to be imaginative, absent-minded, impractical Autia.

Factor N: Privateness- A person obtaining a low Sten score (1-3) is considered to be forthright, open, genuine, Artless; a person obtaining a high score (8-10) is considered to be private, discreet, shrewd, diplomatic, shrewd.

Factor O: Apprehension- A person obtaining a low Sten score (1-3) is considered to be self-assured secure and self-satisfied, whereas a person obtaining high score (8-10) is considered to be self-doubting, self-blaming, guilt -prone, insecure etc.

Factor Q1: Openness to change – A person obtaining a low Sten score (1-3) is considered to be conservative, traditional, whereas a person obtaining a high score (8-10) is considered to be open to change, experimenting liberal critical etc.

Factor Q2: Self Reliance – A person obtaining a low Sten score (1-3) is considered to be group oriented follower, whereas a person obtaining a high score (8-10) is considered to be self-reliant, individualistic, prefers own decisions etc.

Factor Q3: Perfectionism – A person obtaining a low Sten score (1-3) is considered to be lax, tolerates disorders, and flexible, whereas a person obtaining a high score (8-10) is considered to be organized, socially precise, self-disciplined.

Factor Q4: Tension- A person obtaining a low Sten score (1-3) is considered to be relaxed, tranquil, composed whereas a person obtaining high score (8-10) is considered to be tense, frustrated and high energy driven.

Methods and Procedure: Arrangement: Two chairs were positioned in the line 'L' position. The room was well ventilated with open windows so the light and air can be easily passed. A table was placed next to the subject for him to use it to write on. Then the following instruction was given.

Instruction:

"Please read the question carefully. For each question, you must shade the corresponding number in the answer sheet. There are three answers to each question and the test result will be more authentic if you answer in the "uncertain "category as little as possible. There are no right or wrong answers, so try not to think too much about the question and answer them with honesty. Your answer will be kept confidential."

Test Administration:

The subject was given a 16 PF questionnaire and the answer sheet. He was then asked to shade in the corresponding box of the answer sheet. After giving instructions about the test, the subject started to mark his answer in the answer sheet. Then the subject was asked how he felt about the test after finishing the test.

Projective Techniques:

Project methods are based on the projective hypothesis, derived from Freud's personality theory. The basic idea is that the way people respond to a vague or ambiguous situation is often a projection of their underlying feelings and motives.

Thematic Apperception Test: (TAT)

The Thematic Apperception Test, or TAT, is a type of projective test that involves describing ambiguous scenes. Popularly known as the "picture interpretation technique," it was developed by American psychologists Henry A. Murray and Christina D. Morgan at Harvard University in 1935. To date, the TAT is one of the most widely researched and clinically used Personality tests. The TAT consists of 20 pictures all black and white that are shown to a client.

How the TAT Works

The TAT involves showing people a series of picture cards depicting a variety of ambiguous characters (that may include men, women, and/or children), scenes, and situations.

They are then asked to tell as dramatic a story as they can for each picture presented, including:

- what has led up to the event shown

- what is happening in the scene

- the thoughts and feelings of characters

- the outcome of the story

The complete version of the TAT includes 31 cards. Murray originally recommended using approximately 20 cards and selecting those that depicted characters similar to the subject.

Today, many practitioners only utilize between 5 and 12 cards, often selected because the examiner feels that the scene matches the client's needs and situation.2

Practitioners use their best judgment when selecting scenes in order to determine which might be most likely to elicit useful information from the respondent.

Scoring and Interpretation:

Scoring and interpretation. Originally Murray analysed the contents of the stories according to needs and pressures in the form of the environmental forces to which the subject is exposed. The terms of analysis have now been modified and the system of scoring and interpretation takes the following into account:

Hero of the story: What type of personality does he have?

Theme of the story: What is the nature of the theme or plot used in making up the story?

The style of the story. The length of the story, the language used, whether the expression is direct or indirect, forced or poor, organization of the contents, originality and creativity, etc.

The content of the story. What interests, sentiments, attitudes they depict, whether behaviour has been expressed in real terms or as fantasy and what inner state of the mind the story reveals.

Test situation as a whole. The subject's reaction is to be listed as a whole.

Particular emphasis or omissions. The omissions, addition, distortion and attention to particular detail.

Subject's attitude towards authority and sex.

Outcome. Whether the ending of the story is happy, unhappy,funny etc.

As a whole, the recurring themes and features contribute more towards the interpretation than a single response. Moreover, the global view of one's personality should be based on the response of all the twenty pictures shown to the subject. There are many chances of misinterpretation of the contents of stories by an immature examiner. The future of TAT therefore, hangs more on the success in perfecting the interpreter than on success in perfecting the material. People entrusted with interpreting the test must be given adequate opportunities to acquire the necessary knowledge and training for this purpose.

Why the TAT Is Used

The TAT can be utilized by therapists in a number of different ways. Some of these include:3

- To learn more about a person. In this way, the test acts as something of an icebreaker while providing useful information about potential emotional conflicts the client may have.

•	To help people express their feelings. The TAT is often used as a therapeutic tool to allow clients to express feelings in a non-direct way. A client may not yet be able to express a certain feeling directly, but they might be able to identify the emotion when viewed from an outside perspective.

•	To explore themes related to the person's life experiences. Clients dealing with problems such as job loss, divorce, or health issues might interpret the ambiguous scenes and relating to their unique circumstances, allowing deeper exploration over the course of therapy.

•	To assess someone for psychological conditions. The test is sometimes used as a tool to assess personality or thought disorders.

•	To evaluate crime suspects. Clinicians may administer the test to criminals to assess the risk of recidivism or to determine if a person matches the profile of a crime suspect.

•	To screen job candidates. This is sometimes used to determine if people are suited to particular roles, especially positions that require coping with stress and evaluating vague situations such as military leadership and law enforcement positions.

Inkblot test:

History: One of Hermann Rorschach's favorite games as a child was Klecksography, which involves creating inkblots and making up stories or poems about them. He enjoyed the game so much that his school friends nicknamed him "Klecks," the German word for "inkblot."

His interest in inkblots continued into adulthood. While working in a psychiatric hospital, Rorschach noticed that patients with schizophrenia responded to the blots differently from patients with other diagnoses. He began wondering if inkblots could be used to create profiles for different mental disorders.

So, inspired perhaps by both his favorite childhood game and his studies of Sigmund Freud's dream symbolism, Rorschach developed a systematic approach to using inkblots as an assessment tool.

Rorschach wasn't the first to suggest that a person's interpretation of an ambiguous scene might reveal hidden aspects of that individual's personality. Alfred Binet also experimented with the idea of using inkblots as a way to test creativity and originally planned to include inkblots in his intelligence tests.

Uses

The Rorschach test has grown to be one of the most popularly used psychological tests. It's primarily used in psychotherapy and counseling.

Those who use it regularly do so as a way of obtaining a great deal of qualitative information about a person, including their personality, emotional functioning, and thinking patterns. The therapist and client can then further explore some of these issues during therapy.

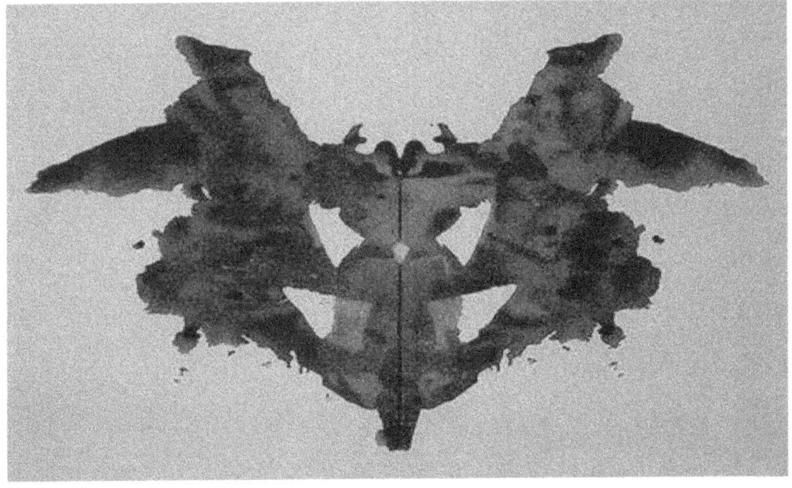

Inkblot

Administration

There are 10 official inkblots, each printed on separate white cards. Five inkblots are black and gray; two are black, gray, and red; and three are multicolored without any black.

During administration, the examiner will sit next to you. This helps them see what you see. The test involves certain steps:

1.   Present: The examiner will give you one card at a time and ask you, "What might this be?"

2.   Respond: You're free to interpret the ambiguous image however you want. You can take however long you like to interpret each card and can give as many responses as you want. You can also hold the cards in any position, whether it is upside down or sideways.

3.   Record: Your examiner records everything you say, no matter how trivial. They'll note the time taken for each response, the position the card is being held, your emotional expressions, etc. during the test.

4.   Confirm: Once you go through all the inkblots once, your

examiner will take you through each inkblot a second time. The goal of this is not to get new information, but to help your examiner see what you see. They'll ask you to identify where you see what you originally saw and what features make it look like that.

On average, it takes about 1.5 hours to administer and score the test.

Scoring

So what exactly do interpreters of the Rorschach test look for when they are analyzing responses to the inkblots? The actual content of the responses is one thing, but other factors are essential as well.

Content

Content refers to the name or class of objects used in your responses. Some common contents include:

•   Whole Human (H): A whole human figure.

•   Human Detail (Hd): An incomplete human form (e.g., a leg) or a whole form without a body part (e.g., a person without a head).

- Human Detail (fictional or mythological; Hd): An incomplete fictional or mythological human figure (e.g., wings of an angel).

- Animal Detail (Ad): An incomplete animal form (e.g., cat's head, claw of a crab).

- Sex (Sx): Anything involving sex organs, activity of a sexual nature, or sexual reproduction (e.g., sexual intercourse, breasts).

- Nature (Na): Anything astronomical or weather-related (e.g., sun, planets, water, rainbow).

Some responses are quite common, while others may be much more unique. Highly atypical responses are notable since they might indicate disturbances in thought patterns.

Location

Identifying the location of your response is another element scored in the Rorschach system. Location refers to how much of the inkblot you used to answer the question.

- "D" if a commonly described part of the blot was used.

- "Dd" if an uncommonly described or unusual detail was used.

- "S" if the white space in the background was used.

- "W" if the whole inkblot was used to answer the question.

Determinants

Determinant coding is one of the most complex features of scoring Rorschach. This is where the examiner considers the reasons why you see what you see. What inkblot features helped determine your response and how?

There are six broad categories of inkblot determinants you could be responding to:

- Color

- Form

- Movement

- Pairs and Reflections

- Shading

For example, if you report seeing a flower in Card 8 because of the red color, your examiner may code that response as Color determinant.

Each category has its own subcategories and there are at least 26 possible determinant codes. More than one determinant can be used in a single response.

Interpretation

Interpreting a Rorschach record is a complex process. It requires a wealth of knowledge concerning personality dynamics generally as well as considerable experience with the Rorschach method specifically.

In addition to formal scores, Rorschach interpretation is also based on behaviours expressed during the testing, patterns of scores across responses, unique or consistent themes in the responses, and unique or idiosyncratic perceptions.

A relatively fast response might indicate being at ease with others and comfortable with social relationships. A delayed response, however, might reveal that the individual struggles with social interactions.

Criticism

Despite its popularity, the Rorschach is a controversial test. Many of the criticisms center on how the test is scored and whether the results have any diagnostic value.

Glossary of Terms

Personality: Individuals unique and relatively stable patterns of behaviour, thoughts and feelings.

Type: A type is a group of correlated traits.

Traits: specific dimensions along which individuals differ in consistent, stable ways.

Secondary Traits: According to Allport, traits that exert relatively specific and weak effects on behaviour.

Central Traits: According to Allport, five to ten traits that best describe an individual's personality.

Cardinal Trait: According to Allport, a single trait that dominates an individual's entire personality.

Psychoanalysis: The method of treating psychological disorders devised by Freud---is to bring repressed material back into consciousness. Presumably once such material is made conscious and patients gain insight into the early life experiences that caused them to repress it in the first place, important causes of mental illness are removed.

Id: In Freud's theory the portion of personality concerned with immediate gratification of primitive needs.

Ego: In Freud's theory the part of personality that takes account of external reality in the expression of instinctive sexual and aggressive urges.

Superego: According to Freud, the portion of human personality represents the conscience.

Anxiety: Unpleasant feelings of tension or worry experienced by an individual.

Defense Mechanism: Technique used by the ego to keep threatening and unacceptable material out of consciousness, and so to reduce anxiety.

Collective Unconscious: In Jung's theory a portion of the unconscious is shared by all human beings.

Archetypes: According to Jung inherited images in the collective.

UNIT IV

Adolescents Mental Health and Hygiene

Adolescents Mental Health and Hygiene

Adolescence Mental Health and Hygiene

Adolescence can be simply defined as the period of a person's life between puberty and maturity (adulthood) generally the teenage years, but not always. In recent years, research has suggested that adolescence is wider than the teenage years. Girls and boys may start puberty at an earlier age, eight and maybe younger in some cases. Recent research also suggests that adolescence is going on for longer than the teenage years, even into the early twenties.

So when we say adolescence, we do mean just that, the period of time in a person's life from puberty to maturity (adulthood).

For humans, it is not merely something discussed in scientific terms, but rather an important social phase in a person's life. Sooner or later after puberty, a person will be expected to take on adult responsibilities. The time that this occurs will depend on the culture in which he/she lives. Adolescence is a universally recognised phase often marked by instruction and ceremony throughout the world. Formal ceremonies tend to be rarer today, but they still occur. For example, certificates for leaving school.

In Western society, pre-adolescent children expect to be cared for by their parents or caregivers, whilst post-adolescent children are expected to be more responsible for their own physical, emotional, intellectual health and their own legal responsibilities.

Adolescence is often a period of crisis for the young person and his/her family.

Adolescence and the idea of teenagers is a relatively new concept. Prior to education for all, people were adults or children. However, since the 1950s, the idea of a teenager has developed. Adolescence is a time of great transition, physically, mentally and emotionally for a child, as they move from childhood to adulthood.

Definitions of Adolescence:

Adolescence is an important period. Adolescence is a complex and often difficult period in development both for adolescence and for their families because of rapid physical change, psychological and cognitive changes and by an accelerating succession of urgent societal demands, adolescence faces formidable challenges in the essential task of deciding who they are, what they are going to be and how they are going get these. Thus, this is an important period of human life.

Adolescence is a transitional period

Adolescence is a period of transition and rapid change. Neither the person is called a child nor an adult because the individual has crossed childhood and yet to reach the stage of adulthood. Thus the status of the individual is vague and diffused and there is confusion about the roles he/she is going to play. Sometimes his innocent behaviour is either called 'childish' or 'too big for his age.

Adolescence is a period of change

It is a general characteristic of the adolescence period. During this stage, there is a change in physical, psychological and sociological aspects of an individual along with values, attitudes, interest and behaviour. Thus consistency and inconsistency are found out in the life cycle.

Adolescence is a period of egocentric and problem age

The sudden and rapid change of physical and psychological aspects during this stage create a problem for the adolescent. Adolescent youth are interested to solve their problem independently and try to achieve independence from parents, cooperative and workable relationships with peers and prepare for a meaningful vocation. But sometimes they cannot solve the problem, which itself creates a problem for them.

Adolescence is a time of the search for identity

Each of the periods has its problems that must be solved if the individual is to enter the next period without handicap. Adolescence is perhaps no more important stage of development than any others, but it is the last stage before adulthood and it, therefore, offers to both parents and teacher the last opportunity to educate a child for his adult responsibility.

During this period adolescents begin to search for their identity and try to develop individuality in their way which sometimes leads to an identity crisis in some adolescence.

Adolescence is a period of unrealism

During this period the aspirations, thoughts and achievement etc are more idealistic rather than realistic. The young boys and girls think the more unrealistic, false and illogical ideas which sometimes hurt and disappoint them in life. It is found out that the false idealistic ideas disappear gradually and adolescence sees their life, family and friends more realistically.

Adolescence is a period of Hero-worship and sexual maturity

During this period the boys and girls consider themselves the hero and heroine of the life cycle. They think that they can do and undo everything during their life span without understanding the reality of life. The above feelings take place due to sudden sexual development on the part of boys and girls.

Adolescence is a period of intensely emotional

During this period the youth often resulted in intense excitement and deep depression. Sometimes he/she may exhibit a 'know-it-all' attitude. Boys like to be thought big, strong and healthy. Girls desire prettiness. In both the sexes, there is interest in an emphasis on physical attractiveness and good grooming.

Adolescence is a period of sexual delinquency

During this period sexual manifestation may cause self-consciousness and desire for other ties. It is a period of mutual liking, thus homosexual and heterosexual feelings create confusion among the adolescence.

Adolescence is a period of high moral values and sacrifice

During this period high moral values are seen. The adolescent youth like to serve in fairs, festivals, social gathering etc and sacrifice their conveniences for social service due to their high moral feelings.

How To Deal With Common Problems Of Adolescence

Adolescence is not an easy time for children or parents. The only way to deal with needs and problems at this age is to know about them and be ready to face them. Parent-adolescent conflicts that cause insecure and unstable feelings have a linear association with pubertal maturity. Understanding and dealing with these conflicts positively could help your child be more responsible and social (1). Here is our list of the most common problems, and their solutions that adolescents have to deal with.

1. Physical changes

Physical changes happen due to changes in the teenager's hormone levels.

•	Development of full breasts in girls can be awkward in the beginning. Girls may start to feel conscious about their figure.

•	Change of voice and appearance of facial hair in boys is perhaps the most prominent change that takes place during adolescence.

• Acne is one of the major problems.

• Muscle gain sometimes leads to excessive body weight in teens.

• The growth of pubic hair in girls and boys.

• Body odor becomes evident.

• Girls start their periods.

2. Emotional changes and problems

Hormones affect your teenager not only physically but also emotionally.

• Adolescence is the age between adulthood and childhood. Teenagers are often confused about their role and are torn between their responsibilities as growing adults and their desires as children.

• They tend to feel overly emotional (blame it on the hormones). Just about anything and everything can make them happy, excited, mad or angry

• Adolescent girls are vulnerable to crying.

- Mood swings are common among teenage boys and girls.

- Bodily changes result in self-consciousness.

- Children who hit puberty early may even feel weird.

- Feelings of inferiority or superiority may arise at this time.

- Adolescence is the age when sexual feelings arise in youngsters. Feelings and thoughts about sex can trigger a sense of guilt

3. Behavioural changes

Overwhelming emotions can lead to impulsive behaviour, which can be harmful to your child as well as others. Mostly, it is just teen behaviour that will last as long as their adolescence.

- Adolescence is the time when children develop and exercise their independence. This can give rise to questioning the parents' rules (seen as argumentative) and standing up for what they believe is right (seen as stubbornness). Significant developmental change in the brain makes teens moody, tired and difficult to deal with.

- The raging hormones in teenage boys can even push them

to get into physical confrontations. They would also want to listen to loud music.

• As a part of their new-found independence, adolescents may also want to try new things and take risks, resulting in careless behaviour.

• Sometimes, peer pressure and the need to 'fit in' can make them behave in a certain way or develop certain habits that are hard to break.

• Your teen's dressing, hairstyle, and sense of fashion also change, mostly to something that you may not approve of.

• The most troubling behaviour is perhaps your teen hanging out with problem children and adapting to a dangerous lifestyle.

Lying is one of the common teen behavioural issues. Teens may lie to avoid confrontation with parents or out of fear.

4. Substance Use and Abuse

Teenagers are vulnerable and can be easily swayed to the wrong side. Substance abuse is one of the biggest problems that parents of adolescents around the world have to deal with.

- Peer pressure is one of the significant factors that drive adolescents to take up smoking and drinking or to do drugs.

- The tendency to take risk encourages most teens to try smoking or drinking even before they are of legal age.

- What may start as a 'thrill', can become a habit if it remains unchecked.

- If there is somebody who smokes or drinks at home, they can become your teen's role models.

- Poor self-esteem and the need to be 'cool' can push adolescents to smoke or drink.

- Easy access to substances like cigarettes, alcohol, drugs, and anabolic steroids may increase the temptation to try illicit substances.

5. Educational challenges

High school is not all about fashion, friends, and parties. Children also have a lot of educational activities on their plate.

- Pressure to perform academically and obtain college admission can be stressful and make your teenager moody.

• Juggling school work, extra-curricular activities (must for college admissions) and chores at home can be tiring.

• Distractions at school can result in poor academic performance, which will add to the pressure.

6. Health problems

Adolescents are vulnerable emotionally and physically. Without proper nutrition and healthcare, they are susceptible to illnesses. According to a 2015 WHO report, 1.3 million adolescents died in 2015, a majority of them had preventable diseases.

• Teenagers have a hectic schedule as they hop from one activity to another with little time to eat or rest properly. Unhealthy eating habits prevent them from getting the nutrition they need.

• Consciousness about their body can lead to eating disorders, especially in girls. Adolescent girls who worry about their weight and appearance can develop disorders like anorexia or bulimia.

• Stress can also lead to loss of appetite and sleeplessness in young children.

• Unhealthy eating habits and a less active lifestyle could

also lead to obesity – this is often the case when your child consumes a lot of empty calories through fast food and sodas.

7. Psychological problems

Research has revealed that around 50% of mental health disorders that adults have, begin at the age of 14. In fact, one-third of adolescent deaths are suicides triggered by depression . If your child is overly moody and is not eating or sleeping at all, it is imperative you get professional help for them.

The most common mental health disorders observed during adolescence are anxiety and mood disorders. Social phobias and panic disorders are common among this age group. Girls may tend to have more vulnerability to develop depressive disorders than boys .

•   Teenagers may have self-esteem or confidence issues. The feelings of inferiority or superiority often arise from their appearance, and acceptance of their body – skin color, beauty, and figure.

•   Poor performance in academics and low IQ can also demotivate them. They develop the 'I'm not good enough' attitude towards life.

• Depression is one of the common psychological problems associated with adolescence.

• The stress and pressure of adolescence can create anxiety related issues, while mood swings can lead to conduct disorder or oppositional defiant disorder.

• Eating disorders are also psychosomatic as they start with the adolescent having a poor self-image and the need to change the way they look by any means

8. Social problems – dating and relationships

Attraction to the opposite sex begins during puberty. Adolescence is the time when their sexual or reproductive organs start developing. At such a vulnerable time, it is but natural for teens to feel awkward in social situations.

• Teenagers want to have an identity of their own. They tend to look up to role models at home or outside.

• Adolescents also start thinking about what is 'right' and 'wrong' and question your take on certain things.

• They need time to understand and get comfortable with their sexuality. Girls and boys start experiencing 'weird' feelings towards the other sex and may not know what to do about it.

•	This is the time they start dating. Your adolescent may not be comfortable talking to you about it and may go with little information or misinformation they have about it.

•	Competition is another important aspect of a teenager's social life. Your child may compete with her peers in anything and everything. Their spirit of competition speaks a lot about their perception of self – whether they have a positive self-esteem or a negative one.

•	Sexual feelings and thoughts of sex may seem wrong to an adolescent, because of which they may feel guilty.

•	Their social circle expands during this time as they seem occupied interacting with friends on social media sites, through their phone and outside.

09. Addiction to cyberspace

The advent of social media has changed the way we interact with each other. It has affected teenage lifestyles the most.

•	Your teen may seem to spend hours on the phone, texting, talking or simply playing.

• Adolescents addicted to the internet tend to have fewer friends and a less active social life. They lead solitary lives and are happy browsing the internet for hours.

• Addiction to cyberspace also cuts short their physical activities, resulting in an unhealthy and sedentary lifestyle.

• Internet addiction adversely impacts academic performance.

10. Aggression and violence

Aggression is especially a concern with adolescent boys. Young boys start to develop muscles, grow tall and have a coarser, manly voice. In addition to that, they are moody and vulnerable and can let others get under their skin.

• Adolescent boys can get into fights at school.

• Worse, they could start bullying others, which is a major problem that adolescent boys and girls have to deal with.

• Boys may fall into bad company and be drawn to acts of violence, vandalism, and aggression. They could be easily swayed to own or use a firearm or a weapon too.

• Impulse acts of violence can lead to serious consequences, including death. According to the WHO report, interpersonal violence causes around 180 adolescent deaths around the world.

• Teenage girls are likely to suffer violence or aggression by a partner

Role of education/teachers in solving problems of adolescents

1 To have the proper knowledge of adolescent's psychology:

A teacher should have knowledge about adolescent's psychology. e 1 What are the specific needs of adolescents? What type of changes take place during this period? What are the problems faced by adolescents? How should they be treated?

2. Provide a suitable environment for proper growth: Adolescence is the stage where maximum growth takes place. They must be provided with a balanced diet. They must be given knowledge of health, personal hygiene, cleanliness, various diseases and their prevention.

3. Rendering proper sex education: the Rapid physiological changes, the secretion of sex hormones, all necessitate the provision of adequate sex information and education for

adolescents.

4. Proper dealing with the adolescents: they should not be underestimated.

5. Training of emotions and satisfaction of emotional needs: the age of adolescence is marked by too much intensity, force, instability and immaturity of emotions. Their emotions should be properly trained and diverted towards the constructive sides.

6. To take care of special interests of the students: The curriculum should provide the open choice of various subjects and activities according to tasks and temperament of the adolescents.

7. Providing Religious and moral education.

8. Provision of vocational education: the strong need of today is to provide job-oriented and vocation based practical education for adolescents.

9. Arranging guidance services.

What Is Mental Health

Mental health includes our emotional, psychological, and social well-being. It affects how we think, feel, and act. It also helps determine how we handle stress, relate to others, and make choices. Mental health is important at every stage of life, from childhood and adolescence through adulthood.

Over the course of your life, if you experience mental health problems, your thinking, mood, and behaviour could be affected. Many factors contribute to mental health problems, including:

- Biological factors, such as genes or brain chemistry

- Life experiences, such as trauma or abuse

- Family history of mental health problems

Mental health problems are common but help is available. People with mental health problems can get better and many recover completely.

Early Warning Signs

Not sure if you or someone you know is living with mental health problems? Experiencing one or more of the following feelings or behaviours can be an early warning sign of a problem:

- Eating or sleeping too much or too little

- Pulling away from people and usual activities

• Having low or no energy

• Feeling numb or like nothing matters

• Having unexplained aches and pains

• Feeling helpless or hopeless

• Smoking, drinking, or using drugs more than usual

• Feeling unusually confused, forgetful, on edge, angry, upset, worried, or scared

• Yelling or fighting with family and friends

• Experiencing severe mood swings that cause problems in relationships

• Having persistent thoughts and memories you can't get out of your head

• Hearing voices or believing things that are not true

• Thinking of harming yourself or others

• Inability to perform daily tasks like taking care of your kids or getting to work or school

Learn more about specific mental health problems and where to find help.

Mental Health and Wellness

Positive mental health allows people to:

- Realize their full potential

- Cope with the stresses of life

- Work productively

- Make meaningful contributions to their communities

Ways to maintain positive mental health include:

- Getting professional help if you need it

- Connecting with others

- Staying positive

- Getting physically active

- Helping others

- Getting enough sleep

- Developing coping skills

What is mental hygiene?

Mental hygiene is the practice of trying to maintain mental health through proactive behaviour and treatment.

Mental health is "one's overall psychological well-being." Hygiene refers to methods for preserving health. (In the popular sense, it refers to things like brushing your teeth and washing your hands.) In this way, mental hygiene is what you do to keep your mind healthy.

Practicing mental hygiene is an ongoing process. Understanding what it is and how to practice it can help improve your quality of life

Characteristics of mental health

Life Satisfaction

A person's ability to enjoy life is frequently used as an indicator of mental health and wellness. It is often defined as the degree to which a person enjoys the most important aspects of their life.

Some factors that have been found to play an important role in life satisfaction include the absence of feeling ill, good relationships, a sense of belonging, being active in work and leisure, a sense of achievement and pride, positive self-perceptions, a sense of autonomy, and feelings of hope.

Resilience

The ability to bounce back from adversity has been referred to as "resilience."People who are resilient also tend to have a positive view of their ability to cope with challenges and seek out social support when they need it. Those who are more resilient are better able to not only cope with stress but to thrive even in the face of it.

Support

Social support is important to good mental health. Loneliness has been shown to have a number of negative health effects. It has been linked to problems with both physical and mental health including cardiovascular disease, depression, memory problems, drug misuse, alcoholism, and altered brain function.

Decreases in social support caused by life changes such as going to college, facing social adversity, changing jobs, or getting divorced can have a negative impact on mental health.

Fortunately, research suggests that it is not necessarily the number of supportive connections you have that it is the most important; it is the quality of these relationships that matters.

Flexibility

Having rigid expectations can sometimes create added stress. Emotional flexibility may be just as important as cognitive flexibility. Mentally healthy people experience a range of emotions and allow themselves to express these feelings. Some people shut off certain feelings, finding them to be unacceptable.

Lack of psychological flexibility has been linked to some types of psychopathology, while research suggests that increased flexibility is connected to better life balance and improved resilience.

Challenges to Mental Health

The National Alliance on Mental Illness (NAMI) states that an estimated one in five U.S. adults experiences a mental health problem each year.7 There are a number of risk factors that can increase the likelihood that a person may experience poor mental health.

Risks to mental health can include:

- Discrimination

- Exposure to trauma

- Family history of mental illness

- Low income

- Medical illness

- Poor access to health services

- Poor self-esteem

- Poor social skills

- Social inequalities

- Substance use

Some of the factors that can help offer protection against poor mental health include having supportive social relationships, strong coping skills, opportunities for engagement in the community, and physical and psychological security.

How to Reduce the Effects of Stress on Your Life

Maladjustment

Maladjustment is a term used in psychology to refer to the "inability to react successfully and satisfactorily to the demands of one's environment". The term maladjustment can be referring to a wide range of social, biological and psychological conditions.

Maladjustment can be both intrinsic and extrinsic. Intrinsic maladjustment is the disparities between the needs, motivations and evaluations of an individual, with the actual reward gain through experiences. Extrinsic maladjustment on the other hand, is referred to when an individual's behaviour does not meet the cultural or social expectation of society.

The causes of maladjustment can be attributed to a wide variety of factors, including: family environment, personal factors, and school-related factors. Maladjustment affects an individual's development and the ability to maintain a positive interpersonal relationship with others. Often maladjustment emerges during early stages of childhood, when a child is in the process of learning methods to solve problems that occur in interpersonal relationships in their social network. A lack of intervention for individuals who are maladjusted can cause negative effects later on in life.

Causes

Children who are brought up in certain conditions are more prone to maladjustment. There are three main causes associated to maladjustment

Family causes.

Socially, children that come from broken homes often are maladjusted. Feelings of frustration toward their situation stems from insecurities, and denial of basic needs such as food, clothing and shelter. Children whose parents are unemployed or possess a low socioeconomic status are more prone to maladjustment. Parents who are abusive and highly authoritative can cause harmful effects towards psychological needs which are essential for a child to be socially well adjusted. The bond between a parent and child can affect psychological development in adolescence. Conflicts between parent and child relationships can cause adolescents to have poor adjustment. The level of conflict which occurs between a parent and child can affect both the child's perception of the relationship with their parents and a child's self-perception. The perception of conflict between parent and child can be attributed to two mechanisms: reciprocal filial belief and perceived threats. Reciprocal filial belief refers to the love, care and affection that a child experiences through their parent, it represents the amount of intimacy a child has with his or her parent. High levels of perceived conflict between parent and child reduces feelings of empathy, a child may feel isolated and therefore alienate themselves from their parent, this reduces the amount of reciprocal filial belief. Adolescents with lower levels of reciprocal filial belief are known to show characteristics of a maladjusted individual. Perceived threats can be characterized as the anticipation of damage or harm to oneself during an emotional arousing event that induce a response towards stress. Worry, fear and the inability to cope with stress during conflicts are indicators of a rise in the level of perceived threat in a parent and child relationship. Higher levels of perceived threats in a parent- child relationship may exacerbate negative self-perception and weaken the ability to cope, this intensifies antisocial behaviour which is a characteristic associated with maladjustment.

Personal causes.

Children with physical, emotional or mental problems often have a hard time keeping up socially when compared to their peers. This can cause a child to experience feelings of isolation and limits interaction which brings about maladjustment.Emotion regulation plays a role in maladjustment. Typically, emotions are generally adaptive responses which allow an individual to have the flexibility to change their emotion based on the demand of their environment. Emotional inertia refers to "the degree in which emotional states are resistant to change"; there is a lack of emotional responsiveness due to the resistance of external environmental changes or internal psychological influences. High levels of emotional inertia may be indicative of maladjustment, as an individual does not display a typical variability of emotions towards their social surroundings. A high level of emotional inertia may also represent impairment in emotional-regulation skill, which is known to be indicators of low self-esteem and neuroticism.

School related causes

Children who are victimized by their peers at school are more at risk of being maladjusted. Children who are victimized by their peers at school are prone to anxiety and feelings of insecurity. This affects their attitudes towards school, victimized children are more likely to show dislike towards schools and display high levels of school avoidance. Teachers who display unfair and biased attitudes towards children cause difficulties in their adjustment towards the classroom and school-life. Unhealthy and negative peer influence, such as delinquency, can cause children to be maladjusted in their social environment.

Associated characteristics

There are some characteristics that are associated with maladjustments.

• Nervous behaviour. Habits and tics in response to nervousness (e.g. biting fingernails, fidgeting, banging of head, playing with hair, inability to stay still).

• Emotional overreaction and deviation. The tendency to respond to a situation with unnecessarily excessive or extravagant emotions and actions (e.g. avoidance of responsibility due to fear, withdrawal, easily distracted from slightest annoyance, unwarranted anxiety from small mistakes).

• Emotional immaturity. The inability to fully control one's emotion (e.g. indecisiveness, over dependence on others, excessively self-conscious and suspicious, being incapable to work independently, hyperactivity, unreasonable fears and worries, high levels of anxiety).

• Exhibitionist behaviour. Behaviours conducted in attempts to gain attention or to portray a positive image (e.g. blame others for one's own failure, high level of overt agreeableness towards authority, physically hurting others).

• Antisocial behaviour. Behaviours and acts that showed

hostility or aggression to others (e.g. cruelty to others, the use of obscene and abusive language, bullying others, destructive and irresponsible behaviours)

• Psychosomatic disturbances. This can include: complications in bowel movement, nausea and vomiting, overeating, and other pains.

Negative effects

Poor academic performance

Maladjustments can have an effect on an individual's academic performance.Individual who are maladjusted behaviours tend to have a lower commitment to scholastic achievements, which cause poorer test results, higher rate of truancy and increased risk of dropping out of school.

Suicidal behaviour

In cases where a child suffers from physical or sexual abuse, maladjustment is a risk for suicidal behaviour. Individuals with a history of childhood abuse tend to be maladjusted due to their dissatisfaction in social support and the prevalence of an anxious attachment style. Clinical implication suggests that by targeting maladjustment in individuals with history of childhood abuse, the risk of suicidal behaviour may be attenuated.

Symptoms:

(1) Nervousness in the child is exhibited by habitual biting and wetting of lips, nail, biting, stammering, blushing, turning pale, constant restlessness, body rocking, nervous finger movements, frequent urination.

(2) The maladjusted child shows undue anxiety over mistakes, marked distress over failures, absent-mindedness, day-dreaming; he refuses to accept any recognition or reward, evades responsibility, withdraws from anything that looks new or difficult: he has lack of concentration, is unusually sensitive to all annoyances is suitable to work when distracted and has emotional tone in argument and feel hurt when others disagree; he makes frequent efforts to gain attention of the teacher. Such are the emotional overreactions and deviations.

(3) The child, having emotional disorders, is unable to work alone, and rely on his own judgment; he is suffering from complexes; he is unusually self- conscious or over-critical of others, either too docile or too suggestive; such are his characteristic traits exhibiting

his emotional stability.

(4) The child who cannot adjust himself in the school environment shows exhibitionistic behaviour. He tends to tease, push and shove other pupils; he wants to be too funny or over-conspicuous; he is either found bluffing, or refusing to accept any lack of personal knowledge; he agrees markedly with whatever the teacher says or does and shows exaggerated courtesy.

(5) The maladjusted child has behaviour disorders which are generally seen in his antisocial behaviour. He is cruel to others, bullies them, uses obscene language, shows undue interest in sex, tells offensive stories, dislikes school work, resents authority, reacts badly to discipline, runs away from the class, and shows complete lack of interest in school work suddenly. He has psychosomatic disturbances also. When he is emotionally distressed, he begins to vomit or develops constipation and diarrhea or tends to overeat and shows other feeling disturbances.

Conclusion:

Many of these symptoms may be seen in normal children but frequent occurrence of a number of these symptoms indicates that the child is mentally ill or maladjusted.

Adjustment

- The word 'Adjustment' means 'to fit', 'make suitable', 'adapt' etc.

- Adjustment is the process through which a person tries to strike a balance between his requirements (needs, desires, and urges) and varying life situations.

- Webster: "adjustment is the establishment of a satisfactory relationship, as representing harmony, conformance, adaptation or the like".

- C. V. Good: "Adjustment is the process of finding and adopting modes of behaviour suitable to the environment or the changes in the environment".

- Shaffer: "Adjustment is the process by which a living organism maintains a balance between its needs and the circumstances that influence the satisfaction of these needs".

- Adjustment is a process that helps a person to lead a happy and contented life while maintaining a balance between his needs and his capacity to fulfill them.

Nature of Adjustment

- It is a continuous process

- Two-way process

Not only the process of fitting oneself into available circumstances but also the process of changing the circumstances to fit one's needs.

- It is the process of need reduction

- It is an achievement

- It brings happiness, efficiency and some degree of social feelings

- It involves psychological and physiological problems.

Area of adjustment

- Health and physical environment

- Finance, living conditions and employment

- Social and recreational activities

- Sex and marriage

- Social psychological relation

- Personal psychological relations

- Moral and religious

- Home and family

- Future – vocational and educational

- Adjustment to school and college work

- Curriculum and teaching.

Measurement of Adjustment

- Testing techniques

- Projective techniques

- Inventory techniques

- Sociometric techniques

- Scaling techniques

- Bell's adjustment inventory by- Hugh M. Bell

- Asthana's Adjustment inventory – H.S. Asthana.

Characteristics of a Well-adjusted Person

- Awareness of his own strength and limitation

- Respecting himself and others

- An adequate level of aspiration

- Satisfaction of basic needs

- Absence of a critical or fault-finding attitude

- Flexibility in behaviour

- The capacity to deal with adverse circumstances.

- A realistic perception of the world.

- A feeling of case with his surroundings.

- A balanced philosophy of life.

Defense mechanisms

- Also known as Adjustment mechanism and Mental mechanism.

- A defence mechanism is an unconscious psychological strategy adopted by the individual to tackle a frustrating situation.

- It is a learned responses which develop unconsciously to

meet a stress situation

•	It may be defined as any habitual method of overcoming blocks, reaching goals, satisfying motives and maintaining equilibrium.

•	A defence mechanism is a coping technique that reduces anxiety arising from unacceptable or potentially harmful impulses

•	Tension reduction activity

•	Every individual uses his own mechanism to maintain the balance of his personality in the society.

•	Defense mechanism helps the individual to preserve his self-concept and protects him from anxiety.

•	Comer (1992): "According to psychoanalytic theory, these are strategies developed by ego to control unacceptable id impulses and to avoid or reduce anxiety".

•	Morgan at al (2005): "unconscious strategies used to avoid anxiety, resolve conflict and enhance self-esteem".

•	Is the unconscious strategy adopted by an individual to protect from ego, to minimize conflict, and to maintain repression.

Types of Defence Mechanism

1.   **Aggression**

•   It refers to forceful activity that can be in the form of either physical, verbal or symbolic or all three.

•   It arises from the frustration where an individual attempts to hurt or destroy the source of frustration.

•   Extra punitive:- aggressive attitudes frustration to another person

•   Intra punitive: frustration to himself.

2.   **Compensation**

This is a mechanism in which an individual tries to balance or over-up his deficiency in one field by exhibiting his strength in another field.

Ex: a boy who fails in academic subjects may save his self-esteem by distinguishing himself in athletics, girls wore high-heeled shoes.

3.   **Identification**

•   It consists of adopting the feelings, attitudes and achievements of others as one's own.

- Here an individual seeks satisfaction in associating himself in some way in the success of others.

- Ex: children often identify themselves with their parents, film stars, cricket players or political leaders.

4. Projection

- Placing blame for one's own actions or inadequacies on someone or else or circumstances-rather than accepting responsibility for their own actions.

5. Rationalization

- Use of a reasonable excuse or acceptable explanation for behaviour.

- It is a face saving device by which the individual justifies his short-comings, failure and incompetence by giving false reasons.

- kind of excuse making process.

- Ex: a boy who failed in math makes use of rationalization when he says the questions were out of syllabus.

Sour grapes:

- Something we cannot get becomes something we did not

want anyway.

•	Here an individual attempts to rationalize his external conditions rather than upon his own inability.

•	Ex: failure to qualify UGC test, one might say, was a blessing as there are a lot of unemployed UGC Holders.

Sweet Lemonism:

•	This refers to the attitude that what is already achieved is better than something that is usually considered more desirable of others.]

## 6.	Negativism

•	Refuse to co-operate and exhibit rebellious behaviour doing the opposite of what is normally expected.

•	This mechanism by which an individual draws the attention of others.

## 7.	Withdrawal

•	It is retreating from situations which cause difficulties or refusing to face problems to avoid the danger of failure and hence the possible frustration.

8.   Regression

•   It is the mechanism of escape from reality by returning to behaviour appropriate at an earlier age.

•   In this the individual returns to a less mature level of development to save his ego.

•   Ex: an adolescent girl who has been frustrated in fulfilling her needs may cry like a child, an old man, by taking off the good olden days.

9.   Repression

•   An individual forgers by pushing down into the unconscious any thoughts that arouse anxiety.

•   It is an unconscious process where in painful experience, shameful thoughts etc. are removed from the conscious mind by pushing them down to the unconscious mind.

10. Sublimation

•   It involves a process of redirecting socially unacceptable desires along desirable channels.

•   Frustrated sexual impulses are usually sublimated as creative effort in music, art and literature etc.

Ex: unmarried women interested in children may give expression to her repressed maternal urges by becoming a nurse

Glossary of terms

Mental health is "one's overall psychological well-being."

Mental hygiene is the practice of trying to maintain mental health through proactive behaviour and treatment.

Adjustment: is the process through which a person tries to strike a balance between his requirements (need, desires, and urges) and varying life situations.

Maladjustment is a term used in psychology to refer to the "inability to react successfully and satisfactorily to the demands of one's environment".

Stress: A state of mental or emotional strain or tension resulting from adverse or demanding circumstances.

Coping: To deal with and attempt to overcome problems and difficulties.

UNIT V

THEORIES OF DEVELOPMENT

THEORIES OF DEVELOPMENT

Jean Piaget's Theory of development:

Jean Piaget (1970) a Swiss biologist, philosopher, and psychologist, who has developed the most detailed and comprehensive theory of cognitive development. Piaget called his approach Genetic Epistemology. Piaget theory is a stage theory—a type of theory suggesting that all human beings move through an orderly and predictable series of changes.

Let us return to Piaget's theory, and begin by noting that central to it is the assumption- often known as constructivism-that children are active thinkers who are constantly trying to construct more accurate or advanced understanding of the world around them (e.g., Siegler & Ellis, 1996). In other words, from this perspective, children construct their knowledge of the world by interacting with it. How do children build such knowledge? According to Piaget, through two basic processes.

The first of these is **assimilation**, which involves the incorporation of new information or knowledge into existing knowledge structures known as schemas. **A schema** is a kind of "cognitive scaffold"—a framework for holding knowledge and organizing it. The second process is **accommodation**; it involves modification in existing knowledge (schema) as a result of exposure to new information or experiences. Let us have an example: A two-year-old child has seen many different kinds of cats and, on the basis of such experience, has built up a schema for cats: relatively small and four-legged animals. Now she sees a squirrel for the first time and through assimilation includes it in this schema. As she encounters more and more squirrels, however, she begins to notice that they differ from cats in several respects: They move differently, climb trees, have much busier tails, and so on. On the basis of this new experience, she gradually develops another schema for squirrels. This illustrates accommodation--changes in existing knowledge structures resulting from exposure to new information. Piaget believed that it is the tension between these two processes that encourages cognitive development. But don't lose sight of the key fact: According to Piaget, as these changes occur, children are constantly trying to make better and more accurate sense out of the complex world around them. Let's now take a closer look at the discrete stages of cognitive development Piaget described.

SENSORIMOTOR STAGE (FIRST 2 YEARS)

Characterized by incorporation of reflex patterns into intentional movements designed

first only to repeat, later to maintain, and then to produce new changes in the environment; increasing understanding of means-end relationships. Object constancy is achieved, and the beginning of true, 'thought" and internalized problem solving are seen; but the child still operates very much in the here and now.

PREOPERATIONAL STAGE (2 TO 7 YEARS) Characterized by unsystematic reasoning. Impressive development of internal representations and language. Thought characterized by egocentrism, animism, and faulty reasoning about cause-effect relationships. Two substages are below;

Preconceptual Substage (2 to 4 Years) Rapid development of language. Begins to engage in symbolic play. Tends to use classes inaccurately (for example, calls all men "Daddy").

Perceptual, or Intuitive, Substage (4 to 7 Years) "Reasoning" appears but remains centered on appearances rather than implications. Tends to center on the most noticeable aspects of things observed and therefore fails to "conserve" identities in volume, number, and mass. May discover true relationships through trial and error but is unable to think in flexible ways that involve reversibility. Confuses reality and fantasy but tries to test which is which.

CONCRETE OPERATIONAL STAGE (7 TO 12 YEARS) Systematic reasoning appears; thought processes are logical and reversible but limited to a child's area of concrete experience. Alternative strategies are invented (for example, two ways of getting to the store). Can coordinate part-whole, hierarchical classifications. Comprehends conservation of number, mass, and other properties.

FORMAL OPERATIONAL STAGE (12 YEARS ONWARD) Characterized by logic, reasoning from hypothetical propositions, evaluating hypotheses through testing all possible conclusions. Present reality

seen as only one alternative in an array of possibilities. Can think about thinking and uses theories to guide thought.

Kohlberg's Moral Development Theory:

Lawrence Kohlberg a psychologist belonging to the University of Harvard is known for putting the theory of development of moral judgement in the individual right from the years of early childhood.

He has based his theory of moral development on the findings of his studies conducted on hundreds of children from different cultures. Kohlberg asked them In order to determine the stage of moral development participants

consider imaginary situations that raise moral dilemmas for the persons involved. Participants then indicated the course of action they would choose, and explained why. According to Kohlberg it is the explanations, not the decisions themselves, that are crucial, for it is the reasoning displayed in these explanations that reveals individuals' stage of moral development. One such dilemma is as follows:

A man's wife is ill with a special kind of cancer. There is a drug that may save her, but it is very expensive. The pharmacist who discovered this medicine will sell it for $2,000, but the man has only$ 1,000. He asked the pharmacist to let him pay part of the cost now and the rest later, but the pharmacist refused. Being desperate the man steals the drug. Should he have done so? Why?

Let us consider the kind of reasoning that would reflect several of the major stages of moral reasoning described by Kohlberg.

Stages or levels of moral development:

Preconventional level (4to 10): At the first level of moral development, the preconventional children judge morality largely in terms of consequences: Actions that lead to rewards are perceived as good as acceptable; ones that lead to punishment are seen as bad or unacceptable. For example, a child at this stage might say" the man should not steal the drug, because if he does, he will be punished.

The Conventional Level: As children's cognitive abilities increase, Kohlberg suggests, they enter a second level of moral development, the conventional level. Now they are aware of some of the complexities of the social order and judge morality in terms of what supports and preserves the laws and rules of their society. Thus a child at this stage might reason:"It's OK to steal the drug, because no one will think you are bad if you do. If you don't and let your wife die, you will never be able to look anyone in the eye again".

The Post Conventional Level:

Finally, in adolescence or early adulthood many, though by no means all, individuals enter a third level known as the post conventional level, or principled level. At this stage, people judge morality in terms of abstract principles and values rather than in terms of existing laws or rules of society. Persons who attain this stage often believe that certain obligations and values transcend the laws of society. The rules they follow are abstract and ethical, not concrete like the Ten Commandments, and are based on inner conscience rather than on external sources of authority. For example, a person at this stage of moral development might argue for stealing the drug as follows: "If the man doesn't steal the drug, he is putting property above human life; this makes no sense. People could live together without private property, but a respect for human life is essential." In contrast, if they argue for not stealing the drug they might reason: "If the man stole the drug he wouldn't be blamed by others, but he would probably blame himself, since he has violated his own standards of honesty and hurt another.

Erikson's theory of social development:

Erikson's theory is, like Piaget's, a stage theory: It suggests that all human beings pass through specific stages or phases of development. In contrast to Piaget's theory, however, Erikson's is concerned primarily with social rather than cognitive development.

Erikson believed that each stage of life is marked by specific crisis or conflict between competing tendencies. Only if individuals negotiate each of these hurdles successfully can they continue to develop in a normal, healthy manner.

The stages in Erickson,s theory are summarized in Table 1. The first four occur during childhood; one takes place during adolescence; and the final three occur during our adult years.

Erickson's eight stages of psychosocial development:

CRISIS/PHASE	DESCRIPTION
Trust versus mistrust	Infants learn either to trust the environment (if needs are met) or to mistrust it.

Autonomy versus shame and doubt	Toddlers acquire self-confidence if they learn to regulate their bodies and act independently. If they fail or are labeled as inadequate, they experience shame and doubt.
Initiative versus guilt	Preschoolers (aged 3-5) acquire new physical and mental skills but must also learn to control their impulses. Unless a good balance is struck, they become either unruly or too inhibited.
Industry versus inferiority	Children (aged 6-11) acquire many skills and competencies. If they take pride in these, they acquire high self-esteem. If they compare themselves unfavourably with others, they may develop low self-esteem.

Identity versus role confusion	Adolescents must integrate various roles into a consistent self-identity If they fail to do so, they may experience confusion over who they are.
Intimacy versus isolation	Young adults must develop the ability to form deep, intimate relationships with others. If they dont they become socially or emotionally isolated .
Generativity versus self-absorption	Adults must take an active interest in helping and guiding younger persons. If they do not, they may become preoccupied with purely selfish needs.

Integrity versus despair	In the closing decades of life individuals ask themselves whether their lives had any meaning. If they can answer yes, they attain a sense of integrity. If they answer no, they experience despair.

Vygotsky's theory:

A Russian psychologist named Lev Vygotsky developed a theory of cognitive development in children known as Lev Vygotsky's Sociocultural Theory of Cognitive Development.

The main assertion of the Vygotsky theory is that cognitive development in early childhood is advanced through social interaction with other people, particularly those who are more skilled. In other words, unlike Piaget's theory Vygotsky proposed that social learning comes before cognitive development in children, and that children construct knowledge actively.

Vygotsky's Concept of Zone of Proximal Development

Lev Vygotsky is most recognized for his concept of Zone of Proximal Development (ZPD) pertaining to the cognitive development in children.

According to the Vygotsky theory of cognitive development, children who are in the zone of proximal development for a particular task can almost perform the task independently, but not quite there yet. With a little help from certain people, they'll be able to perform the task successfully.

Some factors that are essential in helping a child in the zone of proximal development:

The presence of someone who has better skills in the task that the child is trying to learn. This "someone" is known as a "More Knowledgeable Other"(MKO), which we will discuss below.

The child can receive instructions from the MKO during the learning process.

The MKO can offer temporary support (scaffolding) to the child during the learning process. For example, a five-year-old child knows how to ride a tricycle, but can't ride a bicycle (with two wheels) unless his grandfather holds onto the back of her bike. According to Vygotsky's theory, this child is in the zone of proximal development for riding a bicycle. With her grandfather's help, this little girl learns to balance her bike. After some practising, she can ride the bike on her own.

Vygotsky's concept of Zone of Proximal Development underscores Vygotsky's conviction that social influences, particularly getting instructions from someone, are of immense importance on cognitive development in early childhood. According to Vygotsky's theory, as children are given instructions or shown how to perform certain tasks, they organize the new information received in their existing mental schemas. They use this information as guides on how to perform these tasks and eventually learn to perform them independently.

Vygotsky's Concept of More Knowledgeable Other

Vygotsky's sociocultural theory emphasizes that children learn through social interaction that include collaborative and cooperative dialogue with someone who is more skilled in tasks they're trying to learn. Vygotsky called these people with higher skill levels the More Knowledgeable Other (MKO). MKO could be teachers, parents, tutors and even peers

In our example of the five-year-old girl learning to ride a bike, her grandfather not only holds onto the back of the bike, but also verbally teaches her how to balance her bike. From the little girl's point of view, her grandfather is what Vygotsky would call a More Knowledgeable Other.

Vygotsky's Concept of Scaffolding

Vygotsky's concept of scaffolding is closely related to the concept of the Zone of Proximal Development. Scaffolding refers to the temporary support given to a child by a More Knowledgeable Other that enables the child to perform a task until such time that the child can perform this task independently.

According to the Vygotsky theory, scaffolding entails changing the quality and quantity of support provided to a child in the course of a teaching session. The MKO adjusts the level of guidance in order to fit the student's current level of performance.

To illustrate Vygotsky's concept of scaffolding using our example of the five-year-old learning to ride a bike:

The little girl's grandfather (MKO) may begin by holding onto the back of her bike the whole time that she is on the bike. As the little girl gains more experience, her grandfather may release his hold intermittently. Eventually the girl's grandfather only grabs the bike when he needs to correct her balance. When the girl finally masters the skill, her grandfather no longer needs to hold onto her bike anymore, and the scaffolds can be removed.

A major contribution of Vygotsky's theory of cognitive development in children is the acknowledgement of the social component in both cognitive and psychosocial development. Due to Vygotsky's proffered ideas, research attention has been shifted from the individual onto larger interactional units such as parent and child, teacher and student, brother and sister, etc

The Vygotsky theory also called attention to the variability of cultural realities, stating that the cognitive development of children who are in one culture or subculture, such as middle class Asian Americans, may be totally different from children who are from other cultures. Therefore, it would not be fitting to compare the developmental milestones of children from one culture to those of children from other cultures.

References:

Baron A. Robert and Mishra Girishwar Psychology pearson publication

Cicareli KSaundra and White J. Noland psychology Pearson publication

Morgan T. Clifford,King A. Richard Weisz, John R. and John Schopler (An introduction to Psychology) McGraw Hill Education.

Mangal S.K (advanced Educational Psychology) PHI learning private limited.

Sharma B. N (UGC NET-SET book Surya publications).

Ansari M.S. (UGC NET/SLET Education)

Verywellmind.com and its affiliated sites (collectively, the "Site") are Dotdash Meredith brands.

Kendra cherry (16pf)

https://www.psychologynoteshq.com for Vygotsky theory.